W9-CIE-025

Contents

Introduction

While the Second Vatican Council was in process and its documents were being circulated, either in mimeographed form or through IDOC (International Documentation on the Conciliar Church), interested Catholics were meeting in the United States to reflect on those decrees. As a result of some of those gatherings, especially one held at The Grail in the summer of 1964, came the idea of doing an initial study, gathered from a survey of the administrators of all the religious congregations and orders of Catholic Sisters in the United States, to determine with what resources sisters could respond effectively to the *Decree on Renewal of Religious Life* that the Council was preparing. The Conference of Major Superiors of Women (CMSW) initiated precisely such a report at their fall meeting in 1965, after having heard from a number of their members and from sister scholars who had published relevant position papers the previous June in a book called *The Changing Sister*.

As a sociologist, I was asked to design a Congregational Report and to coordinate a study with the guidance of a fifteen member committee responsible for its planning and evaluation. Because the large Sisters' Survey evolved from this planning the following year and involved over 139,000 individual sisters reporting on their own experience, little public attention was given at the time or since to the initial study that reported on the 437 respondent congregations and accounted for 158,917 sisters through administrative records and opinions. Yet those data, compiled in 1966 laid the groundwork for the Sisters' Survey and for the ensuing interpretive reports on it received by all the participants, 88% of all the religious congregations of women in the United States. The factual information from the 1966 study, recorded comparatively for each congregation with the national totals, provided a foundation for the subsequent chapters of renewal of religious women in the United States. Those data were not published, beyond the mimeographed reports received by each participating group.

In 1982, that 1966 report was replicated and extended, constituting the final survey document in what has now become a twenty year study of renewal of Catholic sisterhoods. This monograph is the first published study comparing the 1966 and the 1982 data. The instruments used to gather it are printed in Appendix II.

This volume is dedicated to the two women who had the vision and the administrative wisdom to recommend the study to the Board of the CMSW in 1965, Sister Mary Luke Tobin, S.L., the president of CMSW at that time, and Sister Mary Daniel Turner, SND de Namur, also then a member of the Board. Their fine leadership and loving kindness have inspired many since those early days of renewal. I want also to express my admiration of the whole board of twenty-six women who, despite their wide differences in perception as to how the renewal should proceed, had consensus that this basic research was needed in the initial stage to provide a groundwork for action and reflection. My appreciation is also expressed to Sister Lora Ann Quiñonez, the present administrator of the LCWR, and to all the administrators of the 342 groups who responded so completely to the 1982 follow-up study, thereby making this report possible. Gratitude also goes to the American Board of Catholic Missions of the National Council of Catholic Bishops which funded the final stage of the study.

Special thanks go to the Sisters with whom I live and who provide for me the support, the space, and the caring that make a tremendous task like this one less a burden and more a vital part of the doing of the mission in which they also believe. None of the final data would exist in a usable form without the careful work of research assistants who, besides the necessary skills, have also those human qualities that make tension-filled tasks, especially meeting deadlines, achievable landmarks along the way. So to Sister Patricia O'Brien, Tracey Weis, and to Suzanne Giroux special gratitude for work well done and colleagueship provided. A final word of deep appreciation goes to the editor and reader, Sister Grace Pizzimenti, SND de Namur, who insists on the fine expression of ideas and to Sister Esther MacCarthy who probes for meaning. Both have provided years of friendly emergency assistance, even being willing to work with numbers when crises called for such an extreme sacrifice.

List of Tables

PART I

1. The sources of data

This report compares data collected by survey from Catholic religious congregations of women in the United States in 1966 and 1982. These data were then examined in comparison with a two year study of revised Constitutions of congregations participating in all stages of the joint surveys. The idea of doing the study, which covers the chronological period from 1950 to 1984 was devised in the summer of 1964 when the draft copy of the *Decree on Renewal of Religious Life* of the Second Vatican Council became available for examination. The Conference of Major Superiors of Religious Women (CMSW) invited the members of their congregations to write position papers, which were presented at the national CMSW meeting in 1965. Under CMSW sponsorship, the congregational questionnaire was developed, distributed and processed in 1966 and reported at the national CMSW meeting of that same year. The second stage of what became an extensive twenty-year longitudinal study was the huge membership survey of 1967 in which 139,000 sisters participated.[1] Its purpose was to determine the readiness of American sisters to implement the directives of the Vatican Council. It was presented to the CMSW at their September meeting of 1967. In 1974 there followed a content analysis of chapter documents of 273 congregations and then, successively, the retest of the 1967 survey in 1980 and, finally, this new congregational report of 1982 which replicates and extends the original document of 1966.[2]

The object of the longitudinal study has been the analysis of changing structures of religious congregations of Catholic sisters in the United States. The causal factors sought were those determining the over-all pattern of response and new initiatives stimulated by the Council documents and the individual differences by congregation. The focus of the research is sisters, that is, women in apostolic congregations; nuns, that is those in cloistered contemplative orders are not included (Neal, 1984). The

[1]Although over 139,000 sisters participated, most of the analysis in the Sisters' Survey of 1967 was done with a population of 135,109. The tape today has the larger number so all the more advanced analysis includes all cases returned. Besides the several already published reports on these data, an extended analytic study is now in process. The earlier published reports by the author chronologically include:

"A Progress Report: CMSW Research Committee on Religious Life" in *Proceedings of the CMSW Annual Assembly.* Washington, D.C.: CMSW Secretariat. 1966. 84-86.

"Implications of the Sisters' Survey for Structural Renewal," *Proceedings of the CMSW Annual Assembly.* Washington, D.C. CMSW Secretariat. 1967. 1-33.

"Factors Currently Influencing the Spirit and Structure of Religious Communities," *Pro Mundi Vita.* 16, 1967. 18-22.

"The Signs of the Times and the Implementation of Chapter Decrees," *Proceedings of the CMSW Annual Assembly.* Washington, D.C.: CMSW Secretariate, 1968. 61-82.

"Implications of Sisters' Survey in Regard to Community Life," in *Renewal Through Community and Experimentation.* Canon Law Society of America. 1968.

1982 data include information on membership, entering and leaving trends, availability for apostolic works, administrators' perceptions of reasons for leaving, old and new ministries, life styles, ownership of buildings, professional preparation of sisters, evaluation of candidates for admission, formation programs, participation in government, some preferred sources for information and learning, new apostolic perspectives, constitutions, and general characteristics of participating congregations.

"Stirrings in Religious Life," *Sister Formation Bulletin*, Vol. XVI, No. 1, Fall, 1969. 7-13.

"The Future of the Missionary Sister," *The Church as Mission*. London: Geoffrey Chapman. 1969.

"Final Report of the Survey for Contemplatives," New Malleray Abbey, Dubuque, Iowa. 1970.

"A Theoretical Analysis of Renewal in Religious Orders in the U.S.A.," *Social Compass*. Vol. XVIII, 1971. 7-27.

"The Relation between Religious Belief and Structural Change in Religious Orders: Some Evidence," *Review of Religious Research*. Part I, Vol. XII, No. 1, Fall, 1970. 2-16; Part II, Vol. XII, No. 3, Spring, 1971. 154-164.

"Cultural Patterns and Behavioral Outcomes in Religious Systems: A study of religious orders of women in the U.S.A.," Lille, France: International Conference of Sociology of Religion. 1975. 59-77.

"The Social Environment: Unmasking our Ministry," LCWR Newsletter, Vol. 9, No. 1. December, 1980. 7-8.

"The Sisters' Survey, 1980," *Probe*. National Association of Religious Women, May/June, 1981.

[2]Other related surveys, using the same instrument or a modified form, include the Contemplative survey of 1971, with fifteen orders of men and women participating; the international Notre Dame de Namur survey taken in five different languages in 1967, the South African school study, done in 1971 and a Jesuit survey including the two western provinces in 1968. Except for the Jesuit study, this author was the chief investigator.

2. Membership

The opening theme of this analysis is that of declining membership, a reality already manifest in its incipient stage in 1965, as evidenced by the fact that two and a half pages of questions in the original questionnaire of 1966 were devoted to the phenomena of entering, leaving, retiring, and illness. (See 1966 questionnaire in Appendix II, Items 12, 15-21, 55-62.) The basic data are that there are 40% fewer sisters today than there were in 1966, 31% fewer sisters in final vows, and 86% fewer in preparation for final vows. How they distribute can be seen on Table I.

TABLE I
MEMBERSHIP IN CATHOLIC SISTERHOODS
IN THE UNITED STATES

	1966	% of membership	1981	% of membership	'66-'81 shift
Final vows	145239	84	100615	96	−30.7%
Initial commitment	13588	8	1932	2	−85.8%
Novices	7257	4	780	1	−89.2%
Affiliates	4376	3	642	1	−85.3%
Candidates	3406	2	569	1	−83.3%
Totals	173866		104538		
Missing data	24000	(13.8%)	26000	(24.8%)	

Table I shows the actual number of sisters in the 342 separate groups who responded to the thirty-two page questionnaire, sponsored by the Leadership Conference of Women Religious (formerly the CMSW) and partially funded by the National Council of Catholic Bishops. The respondents were administrators of pontifical and diocesan congregations with fifty or more members. They represent 104,538 sisters. Summing the membership of the non-responding congregations from the National

Catholic Directory, we find another 26,000 sisters. This leads us to conclude that there were actually about 130,000 sisters in the United States in 1982, if one includes all stages of initial membership, as we did. This means that our survey represents 75% of all sisters in the United States. Since we excluded communities of fewer than fifty members, it more accurately represents larger groups.[3]

An early question that comes to mind is this: how many of the women surveyed are presently available for apostolic service?

TABLE II
AVAILABILITY FOR APOSTOLIC WORKS

	1966	% of membership	1981	% of membership	'66-'81 shift
Total members	173866	100.0	104538	100.0	−39.9%
Initial formation	28627	16.5	3923	3.7	−86.3%
Over 65	30105	17.3	39402	37.7	+30.9%
Inactive: illness	5738	3.3	6532	6.2	+13.8%
Inactive: old age	8357	4.8	17822	17.0	+113.3%
Total inactive	14095	8.1	24354	23.3	+72.8%

Our data tell us that where 17% were over sixty-five in 1966, today 38% are. Of course, not all of these sisters are inactive. In 1966, 8.1% of all sisters were inactive; today, 23.3%. Thus, if we were attempting to replace the sisters of 1966 today, it would be impossible. The replacement level is down 159%. But, as we shall see, in proceeding through the data gathered, replacement in ministry may well not be the purpose of religious life today.

---

[3] The orders of contemplative nuns constitute about 4000 more women not included here.

3. Entering and leaving trends

Before pursuing that theme further, we have one other membership trend to examine, that of the decline in numbers entering and the increase in the number leaving.

TABLE III

ENTERING TRENDS FROM 1950 THROUGH 1980

	Number entering	Number making final vows	% entrance group making final vows
1948-1952	23302	16320	70%
1953-1957	27157	18168	67%
1958-1962	32433	No data	—
1963-1965	18316	No data	(2 year span)
1966-1970	8699	4408	51%
1971-1975	2590	1986	77%
1976-1980	2767	Incomplete time span	

In Table III, the data for 1950 through 1965 were collected in 1966; from 1966 to 1980, in 1982. Where the data are missing, they were not available because, at the time the information was gathered, the period of initial commitment was not yet completed. From this Table, you can see the dramatic decline in the actual numbers entering: 23,302 between 1948 and 1952; 27,157 from 1953 to 1957; 32,433 between 1958 and 1962; and, then, only 8,699 between 1966 and 1970; 2,590 between 1971 and 1975; and 2,767 between 1975 and 1980, the latter statistic denoting a slight increase. According to a report in *Origins*, (November 17, 1983, p. 395), the number of women novices in the world went up from 11,049 to 14,772 between 1976 and 1980, indicating that about 20% of all entrances world-wide came from the United States. But although the world increase is 25%, the United States increase is only 7%. Furthermore, in the United States, besides the decline in the number entering, there is also, until recently, an increase in the number leaving.

TABLE IIIa
LEAVING TRENDS FROM 1950 THROUGH 1980

	Number leaving	Before final vows	After final vows
In 1950	381	no data	no data
In 1955	590	no data	no data
In 1960	765	no data	no data
In 1965	1562	no data	no data
In 1966	2015	1177	838
In 1970	4337	1723	2614
In 1976	1191	294	897
In 1980	751	147	604

An examination of Table IIIa reveals that the numbers leaving rise from an annual 381 in 1950 to 1,562 leaving in 1965; 2,015 in 1966; and 4,337 in 1970. The trend declines again to 1,191 leaving in 1971 and 751 in 1980. The total number leaving between 1966 and 1981 was 31,763; the number transferring from one congregation to another, 541.

4. *Why members leave*

Whatever the causal factors, the extensive movement is subsiding in the mid-eighties as a new and quite different trend in membership begins. The stark contrast of 34,448 entering and making vows in the nine year period from 1948 through 1957 and only 6,394 in the nine year period 1966 through 1975 is a drop of 81%. This raises the question of why some sisters were leaving and why more were not coming. We cannot find out from sisters why new members were not coming, but we can and did ask administrators both in 1966 and again in 1982 why they thought some were leaving.

Asked to choose from a set of precoded responses (derived from earlier interviewing) why they thought sisters were leaving, the 423 responding administrators in 1966 and the 342 in 1982 ranked respondents somewhat differently if they left before making their perpetual vows than if they left after perpetual vows. Table IV shows these interpretive differences, as well as the differences by years. Only the top six choices are shown in both cases.

TABLE IV
REASONS FOR LEAVING AS PERCEIVED BY ADMINISTRATORS IN 1966 AND IN 1982

Before final vows (BFV)	1966	1982
No vocation	47%	65%
No personal fulfillment	31%	51%
Prefers marriage	33%	49%
Dissatisfaction with community life	40%	49%
New appreciation of lay role	Not asked	20%
Psychological disturbance	41%	8%
After final vows (AFV)	**1966**	**1982**
Dissatisfaction with community life	48%	61%
No personal fulfillment	31%	55%
Prefers marriage	20%	52%
No vocation	16%	33%
Disenchantment with direction of community	Not asked	33%
Psychological disturbance	43%	24%

The choice of answers ranged from "very frequent" to "never." The percentages shown in Table IV are sums of "very frequent" and "frequent." The Table shows that the assumption of "No vocation" is more limited to those under perpetual vows in 1966 but not in 1982. Administrators are more certain that "no vocation" is a major reason for leaving before perpetual vows in 1982 (65%). So too with "failure to achieve personal fulfillment," it is up from 31% to 51%. "Dissatisfaction with community life" is given as a reason for leaving by 40% in 1966 and by 49% in 1982 before perpetual vows, and by 48% and 61% respectively, after perpetual vows. "Preference for marriage" is up 16% as a reason when accounting for those under perpetual vows (49%); but up 32% for the over-perpetual vow group (52%). "Psychological disturbance," used to explain leaving of those over perpetual vows in 1966 (43%), is much less a reason in 1982 (24%). "Disenchantment with the direction of community" ranks fifth in 1982, but was not asked in 1966. This community factor is probably a major explanation today, as we shall see later in this report. (See Appendix I, Tables IVa and IV, for complete data.)

These several reasons are instructive because they show the individual differences associated with individual leavings. Administrators know the leavers personally. In all probability, the over-all trends in numbers leaving are more social than psychic, caused by concomitant trends in the conditions of society and the church's response to them, the changing apostolic needs in relation to population shifts and new calls for prophetic and institutional service. The availability of the laity for many traditional services staffed prior to the Council almost exclusively by religious congregational membership, and the radical shift in the church's definition of ministry, are other contributing causes. Factors of this nature will appear later in this report when we examine new apostolic perspectives.

PART II

1. Works sisters do

We turn now to data concerning current works which sisters are doing, locations at which these works are done, and preparation sisters have for their doing. First, we will examine current works.

TABLE V
WORKS THAT SISTERS DO: A SUMMARY

	1966	% of membership	1982	% of membership
Teaching	92125	58.0%	24179	23.1%
Teaching administration	8978	5.7%	6293	6.0%
Missionary/Catechetical	7471	4.7%	8105	7.7%
Health care	8692	5.5%	5147	4.9%
Health care administration	1767	1.1%	1402	1.3%
Social service	4515	2.8%	3830	3.7%
Staff within congregation	3539	2.2%	3625	3.5%
Staff national organizations	46	.0%	147	.1%
Library services	1569	1.0%	1402	1.3%
Clerical services	2093	1.3%	2291	2.2%
Domestic/other	9153	5.8%	3317	3.2%
Total	139948	88.1%	59738	57.1%
Full time study	1662		1368	
Active retired	21748		21580	
Part time employed	83449		16782	

Table V is only a summary table to give focus to the more extensive data available in Appendix I. From what is included here, we can see that 58% of all professed sisters in 1966 were engaged in full time teaching and another 5.7% in teaching administration. Further breakdown of the data shows that 70% of the teachers taught elementary school.[4] The next highest work commitment was health care with 6.6% of the professed sisters involved, increasing by .2%, if nursing education is included here. Those in pastoral ministry work, including everyone in full time religious education, equalled 2.9%, while all of those in missionary work in foreign countries accounted for 1.7%. Social work occupied 2.8% of the sisters. While just over 2% were engaged in central administration, 1.3% were working in clerical service, and 5.8% in domestic and other internal staff work in the congregations or in diocesan or parish offices. Many others were working part time in these several functions, but their work cannot be calculated by percent of the whole because some sisters were doing their part time job over and above their full time position or had two or more part time jobs. (This phenomenon for 1966 can be examined on the extended Table V in Appendix I.)

The distribution of works is quite different in 1982: school staffing declines from 64% of all work done by sisters to 29.1%, 6% of which is in administration; 6.2% are in health care with another .2%, if nursing education is included; 1.5% are on foreign missions; 6% in pastoral ministry of the standard sort, (double the 1966 percentage); 3.7% are in social services of all kinds; 3.5% are

---

[4]The source of these data is the Sisters' Survey of 1967. The computerized data is available for examination on request to the author at the Sociology Department, Emmanuel College, Boston.

congregational administrators and another 3.2% provide nurturing services for congregations, seminaries and local parishes. All other work done falls into a variety of small categories or is done on a part time basis. By making an equivalent scale for reported part time work, (see Appendix I, Table V), we can conclude that about 6% of all sisters today are unemployed. They are probably looking for work. Being out of work is a category we did not find for sisters in 1966.

Within the data just reported, there are some works that are new for the particular congregations doing them. In order to count these changes in ministries across congregations, and to avoid simply re-naming what had always been done, we asked specifically: what new works have you introduced since 1965 and how many sisters are involved in them? (Items 126 and 127). In another item (119), we asked if new works with a specific justice component had been introduced with the intention of implementing the mandates of *Gaudium et Spes* (1966) and the Bishops' Synod document *Justice in the World* (1971). (This question was asked only in 1982.) Table Va shows the responses:

TABLE Va

NEW WORKS INTRODUCED SINCE 1965

New works in general	% mentioning	Works with a special justice focus	% mentioning
Alleviate poverty	15.8%	Social service/health	38.9%
Parish work	14.9%	Urban/rural poor	33.3%
City work: not schools	9.6%	Social justice work	27.2%
		Hispanic apostolate	10.2%
Systemic change	4.1%	Foreign missions	9.6%
With the disabled	3.5%	With the disabled	7.3%
Other[5]	43.9%	Halfway houses	6.7%

Works with a special justice focus

	% men- tioning
Houses of prayer	5.0%
Renewal centers for laity	2.9%
Other	67.5%

Both of the questions eliciting these responses were open-ended. The administrators reported only 8% of their members in the new works. For works with a social justice direction, 54.7% answered specifically that they had introduced work toward this end and 30.4% said they had not done so (Item 119). This tells us that, although there has been much discussion of new works and much action toward choice of ministry, discussion and action are not moving large numbers of sisters into ministries more consonant with their new mission statements. This will be further developed later.

At this point, we can say that there is a radical decline in the number of sisters in formal teaching: from a unit average of 239 sisters in 1966 to one of 89 sisters in 1982; an average difference of 150 sisters per unit whether that be a province or a congregation. In other words, there are about 49,797 sister teachers now, compared with 97,990 in 1966, a decline of 50.8%, (compared with a membership decline of 40%). We can conclude that most of the sisters who have left were in teaching roles and that most of those moving to new ministries were also. The other ministries were much smaller to begin with and are now within two or three percentage points of what they were before, but, in most cases, in a declining direction. The

---

[5]The category, "other," is a mix of many different works which our code defined as traditional works plus several that yielded deceptively small percentages since the entire set includes only 8% of all sisters being accounted for.

fact that the growing affluent segment of the Catholic population is producing fewer children for the traditional schools and religious education programs is one factor to be pondered while examining these data. It suggests the hypothesis that the sisters who are leaving are predominantly teachers whose replacement is not essential, given immediate needs of elementary and, later, of high schools, the places where the burgeoning vocations were recruited and placed in the 1950's and 1960's. This raises a question about whom and what we had been teaching and whom and what we want to teach now.

2. Places where sisters work

A look at the places where sisters do their work will help us to understand some of the changes that have occurred. In 1966, sisters worked in 15,676 buildings owned and operated by the congregations or by the local church. (See Table VI below.) Ownership of these buildings distributed between the congregations and other organizations, with 19.7% congregational ownership of the places where sisters worked but 3% only of the elementary schools. Sixty-five percent of the buildings where they worked were elementary schools (10,198). Today there are only half that many elementary schools, 5,928 of them, of which only 172 are owned by sisters' congregations. The number of high schools has declined from 2,257 in 1966 to 1,689 in 1982; then, 30% were owned by sisters; now, only 19%. Hospital sites as places of work for sisters has increased 146%.

There has been an increase in the variety of places where sisters work along with a decline in ownership of such places. Sisters worked in 189 colleges in 1966 and owned 85% of them. Today they work in 591 colleges and own 97 of them. This means that 63 of those they owned in 1966 they no longer own now. They are working in three times as many social welfare centers and nursing homes and in twice as many homes for the aged. Employment locations in religious education centers have increased by 676%, from 208 locations to 1,408 places. There is also an increase of 768% of a variety of places of work that do not fit into this standard code, a fact suggesting a diffusion of ministries.

Sisters used to own many more of the health care centers where they worked. This was also true of retreat centers, special schools, child care centers, and homes for children. The elementary schools were always predominantly controlled by the local church, never more than 3% by the sisters.

Today there are 14,673 buildings in which sisters work, owned by either the local church, the sisters' congregations, or the public community. This is a decrease of only 6% in the actual number of locations. The distribution of functions of those buildings is quite different. The elementary schools make up only 40% of the work places now, as compared with 65% in 1966; the high schools, 11.5%, compared with the former 14%. All of this suggests that, though sisters are doing works with the same names as formerly, they are doing them in different settings. As we shall see later, choice of ministry is an accelerating factor in the diffusion of ministries, away from schools particularly. We should keep in mind, however, the question of which schools sisters are moving toward and which ones are being closed by diocesan decisions.

TABLE VI

CONGREGATIONAL OWNERSHIP OF BUILDINGS
WHERE SISTERS WORK

	1966			1982		
	% of type	% of total	Total	% of type	% of total	Total
Pre-school	40.4%	1.0%	408	35.0%	.96%	399
Elementary school	3.1%	2.0%	10198	2.9%	1.00%	5928
High school	30.2%	4.3%	2257	19.0%	2.15%	1688
Junior school	98.3%	.6%	99	34.0%	.20%	89
College	85.0%	1.0%	189	16.0%	.66%	591
Graduate school	80.6%	.1%	21	16.0%	.09%	85
Nursing school	91.4%	1.7%	287	40.0%	.29%	106
Special school	49.1%	.3%	112	22.0%	.35%	233
Religion center	6.1%	.1%	208	1.0%	.10%	1408
Retreat center	90.6%	.6%	98	57.0%	1.28%	331
Hospital	86.2%	4.4%	805	39.0%	3.10%	1182
Clinic	43.2%	.4%	147	31.0%	.30%	160
Nursing home	75.9%	.6%	117	36.0%	.90%	373
Social welfare center	12.4%	.1%	102	5.5%	.10%	308
Maternity/infant center	37.3%	.1%	34	23.0%	.05%	35
Child care center	49.9%	.1%	53	30.0%	.20%	121
Home for orphans	32.8%	.3%	129	24.0%	.05%	33
Home for delinquents	79.8%	.3%	53	50.0%	.20%	58
Home for working women	86.5%	.2%	44	62.0%	.10%	24
Home for aged	76.9%	.8%	165	44.0%	1.00%	364
Guest home	90.6%	.2%	28	80.0%	.30%	50
Community center	Not asked in 1966			40.0%	.10%	50
House of prayer	Not asked in 1966			57.0%	.50%	120
Other	65.8%	.5%	122	14.0%	.90%	937
Total			15676			14673

3. *Professional preparation*

Along with the works that sisters do and the places
where they do them, we should examine the professional
preparation they have acquired for doing their works.

Table VII in Appendix I gives the complete data, but the following summary table presents highlights.

TABLE VII

**PROFESSIONAL PREPARATION OF SISTERS:
ADVANCED DEGREES**

	1966	%	1982	%
Social science	2333	8.7%	3066	6.9%
Languages	1518	5.7%	2067	4.6%
Natural sciences/Mathematics	2783	10.4%	3486	7.8%
Humanities	4514	16.8%	5773	12.9%
Education	8690	32.3%	11323	25.3%
Theology	2283	8.5%	6037	13.5%
Other professions	4741	17.6%	13000	29.0%
Totals	26862	100.0%	44752	100.0%

From the Sisters' Survey data of 1967 with 135,109 sisters responding, we know that 35.4% were college graduates, that is, 51,987; and 21% more or 28,742 had masters' degrees or the equivalent; and 1.7%, that is, 2,362, had doctorates. I cite these data because they record a higher number of degrees than do the congregational reports of 1966 and are probably even more accurate, since each sister in the 1967 questionnaire answered for herself.[6] The congregational reports of 1966 give the total graduate degrees as 25,196 masters and 1,666 doctorates. The statistical discrepancy derives from the imprecision of congregational records maintained at that time, if they were maintained at all. In 1982, there are 98,143 degrees, including bachelors. Of these, 41,828 or 43% are

[6]The Annual Proceedings of the Conference of Major Superiors of Women Religious for 1965, 1966, 1967, 1968 have reports that I made on the original 1966 congregational survey and the Sisters' Survey of 1967. The 1965 issue contains several articles by the people who became the planning committee for the study. They are instructive in setting the vision for the survey.

masters' degrees, and 2,924 or 2% are doctorates. There is a noticeable increase then in the number seeking the professional credential, the master's degree, with only a slight, though doubling numerical rise in those gaining the independent scholar degree, the doctorate. Sisters, at the moment, then, are not planning to create or even to staff extensively their own research centers. But, if this is the case, what are they planning to do?

This question leads us to examine the change, if any, in the kinds of degrees sisters are acquiring and the extent of that change. From Table VIIa (see Appendix I for full table), we can see that education is still the major area of advanced degrees for sisters but, although there are more education degrees now, they are only 25% of all degrees earned by sisters, down 7% from 1966.

TABLE VIIa

TOP TEN FIELDS OF STUDY: ADVANCED DEGREES

	1966	%	1982	%
Education	8690	32.3%	11323	25.3%
Theology/Religious education	2283	8.5%	6037	13.5%
Administration	1104	4.1%	3317	7.4%
English/Literature	2552	9.5%	3246	7.3%
History	1572	5.8%	1988	4.4%
Counseling	532	2.0%	1734	3.9%
Mathematics	1176	4.4%	1462	3.3%
Music	935	3.5%	1295	2.9%
Library science	859	3.2%	1215	2.7%
Nursing	681	2.5%	1145	2.6%
Other advanced degrees	6478	24.1%	11990	26.8%
Total	26862	100.0%	44752	100.0%

On the other hand, theology degrees have almost doubled, from 8.5% to 13.5% in the same sixteen year period. Other professional degrees are up by 197%. Taken together, the liberal arts degrees have increased 164%. The over-all number of advanced degrees earned has increased by 167%. So acquiring professional degrees is increasing.

Looking only at the specific areas of specialization on Table VIIa, where the top ten fields of study are ranked, we can see that education still ranks first, followed by theology and religious education. The only new professional degree that competes with the humanities is counseling. Degrees in this area have doubled since 1966, from 2% to 4%. Nursing has slightly increased and library science is down as percent of total degrees earned.

In 1966, we did not ask the field of concentration for bachelor degrees. Fifty-four percent of all degrees earned since 1966 have been bachelors', and 42% of these in education. (See Appendix I, Table VII). Humanities is second with 18.5% and social science, third with 12.0%. Math and science accounts for only 6.7% and the professional degrees, for 6.1%. Language has only 4.1% and theology 1.5%. None of these statistics indicate any striking change in planned professional training. There are, however, some new directions in professional preparation which, though small in number, are indicators. Table VIIb show those directions.

TABLE VIIb
NEW ACADEMIC SPECIALIZATIONS SINCE 1965

Special administrative training	6224	5.3%
Pastoral ministry	1813	1.6%
Theology/Religious education	1265	1.1%
Health/social service	787	.7%
Spiritual direction	410	.4%
Special education	137	.1%
Gerontology	137	.1%
Communication	68	.1%
Business administration	68	.1%
Justice and peace	34	.0%
Third world	34	.0%

TABLE VIIb (Continued)

NEW ACADEMIC SPECIALIZATIONS SINCE 1965

Urban studies		
Law	34	.0%
Community organization	10	.0%
Other	1470	1.3%
Total	12525	10.8%

For different congregations, different specialties are new, depending, for the most part, on what they were doing in the past and how they were doing it. From the table, it would seem that the major new emphasis is on pastoral ministry, with 1813 new workers studying in that field since 1966. Another 1,265 are newly choosing theology and religious education; and 787, health services. Only thirty-four are especially studying to do justice and peace work; and 68, communication. None of these new direction choices are opted for by many sisters, but this is in itself informative. The fact that 6,224, or 5%, are now getting special administrative training is one of the most important findings in this section.

PART III

1. Credentials of new members

A comparison of the background of candidates for admission in 1966 and in 1982 indicates some clear differences in who is applying for membership, as far as professional credentials are concerned.

TABLE VIII

EDUCATIONAL BACKGROUND OF CANDIDATES

	1966 %	1982 %
No high school diploma	3%	.6%
High school diploma only	79%	12%
Bachelors' degree	4%	41%
Masters' degree	.5%	12%
Doctoral degree	0%	1%
Nursing degree	1%	6%
Social work degree	0%	2%
Other professional degree	0%	6%
Some college	12%	29%
Other post high school training	2%	10%

This table demonstrates a radical change in preparation for admission. In the 1950's, religious congregations introduced a major undergraduate educational program for new candidates. This integrated education replaced the previous thirty year experience of sisters' studying on weekends and during summers to complete academic work for their first degrees, while at the same time, getting their educational methods training as apprentices to skilled sister teachers from within their own or nearby communities of the religious congregations. Such also was the case with nursing, social service, and religious educational training. Comparing 1966 with 1982, we see that the percent entering without a high school diploma has decreased from 3% to less than 1%; the number with only a high school diploma, from 79% to 12%. However, the number of those with a college degree completed prior to entrance has increased from 4% in 1966 to 41% in 1982, with another 12% having already completed the masters' program, compared to only .5% in this category in 1966. Clearly, a message about mission has gone out to new candidates. Only 12.6% are entering without some experience with higher education, and 68% are entering with a higher education credential, 27% of these being beyond the bachelor's degree. This is not, then, due to the decision to take more mature candidates made by many congregations in the renewal period, but to the fact that the candidates who are responding to the religious calling are people with trained competencies in teaching, health work, social services and other fields. It is not only work experience that has been added, but professional training prior to entrance. Is this striking change a result of the new requirements for admission established by religious congregations? I do not think we can conclude this. As Table IX shows, credentials are more demanding, but not to the degree suggested by the change adduced.

TABLE IX
CREDENTIALS REQUIRED FOR ADMISSION

	1966	1982
High school diploma	87.2%	71.1%
Bachelors' or equivalent	.7%	9.6%
Other educational requirements	2.7%	6.1%
Some college	3.1%	42.1%
Some work experience	8.7%	63.7%
Other	3.4%	13.5%

The high school diploma alone was required by 87% of congregations in 1966, and by 71% in 1982. The difference in 1982, however, is that now some congregations (42%) require either some college or some work experience (63.7%) of new candidates, while another 16% require some specific college equivalent. What probably is happening is that direct appeal to joining is currently less emphasized at the high school level. Instead, it has moved to the college level, as sisters come to find the readiness of younger women for the new understanding of mission not quite adequate to the task in hand. At the same time, the formation program of the present is not yet ready to provide the more immediate training for work related to the doing of the mission for which more specific training is needed. The sisters, therefore, look to their professional peers for new colleagues rather than to the students in the schools where only half of them now teach. As sisters strive to develop their own consciousness of the call to a special option for the poor in a way quite different from their old standard ways of thinking of apostolic service, they realize the need of their new colleagues for a commitment to the mission of the church deeper than that expected of candidates prior to the Second Vatican Council and the updating of their own

Constitutions. This will be treated later, when we look at new apostolic perspectives of sisters in 1982.

2. *Procedures for acceptance of candidates*

We turn now to procedures for accepting candidates for admission. The only real differences in procedures are shown on Table X.

TABLE X

CONSULTATION FOR ACCEPTANCE OF CANDIDATES

	1966	1982
Formation personnel	38.7%	80.1%
Provincial council	36.1%	54.7%
Professional psychiatrist	8.0%	7.6%
Professional psychologist	29.1%	55.8%
Medical doctor	76.3%	74.0%
Spiritual director	34.2%	26.6%
Vocation director	31.2%	68.7%
Major superior	17.4%	31.9%
Other	11.9%	20.5%

Our examination of previously used screening procedures in 1966 reveals that the transition to using psychological testing and professional-type interviews had, for most groups, already begun in 1966, as had the elimination of previously enforced restrictions, such as illegitimacy of birth.

It is evident that formation personnel, including vocation director as well as major administrators, are much more involved in accepting candidates today than formerly. The assistance of a psychologist is also a more common practice. This practice suggests a greater care taken in the choice of candidates. It also indicates the professional formalization of procedures for recruitment, and selectivity as to who is recruited.

Still another change is in the length of the formation program. Fifty-four percent of all congregations now allow for the extension of initial commitment through a nine year period. While 10% have eliminated the aspirancy program, another 21.6% have initiated it, as seen in Table XI. An average of 25% have revised the length of all their formation programs.

TABLE XI

EXTENSION OF LENGTH OF FORMATION PROGRAMS IN 1982

	Extended	Revised	Initiated
Aspirancy	10.8%	19.6%	21.6%
Pre-novitiate	25.4%	29.5%	3.2%
Novitiate	17.3%	22.8%	.9%
Temporary commitment	28.4%	27.5%	.3%
Tertianship	.9%	4.7%	1.5%

The amount of time added to each program varies from congregation to congregation and from candidate to candidate. Ceremonies of entrance are not as regimented as they were in the 1950's and 1960's. The aspirancies are for older candidates today.

3. *Qualifications for formation director*

The role of the formation director has had a shift in required qualifications. Table XII identifies these.

TABLE XII

QUALIFICATIONS FOR FORMATION DIRECTOR 1966 AND 1982

	1966	1982
Understanding of psychology	86.7%	Second highest choice
Knowledge of theology	72.4%	Highest choice
Splendid generosity	70.5%	
Regularity of life	65.1%	
Rooted in congregational tradition	59.3%	Fourth highest choice
Pro innovation in liturgy	40.9%	

TABLE XII (Continued)

QUALIFICATIONS FOR FORMATION DIRECTOR 1966 AND 1982

	1966	1982
Personal orderliness	33.4%	
Preserves congregational customs	29.5%	
Pro innovation in community style	16.7%	
Justice orientation and experience	Not asked	Fifth highest choice
Commitment to church mission	Not asked	Third highest choice
Sense of humor	Not asked	
Other	85.7%	

TABLE XIIa

QUALIFICATIONS FOR FORMATION DIRECTOR 1982
Five highest choices

	1	2	3	4	5	Total
Understanding of psychology	20	38	16	9	4	87
Knowledge of theology	29	14	15	9	9	76
Splendid generosity	3	2	8	5	6	24
Regularity of life	2	.3	8	8	2	20
Rooted in congregational tradition	13	14	27	9	6	69
Pro innovation in liturgy	.3	.6	2	3	—	6
Personal orderliness	—	—	.3	—	.6	1
Preserves congregational customs	.6	2	2	3	1	9
Pro innovation in community style	.3	.9	2	4	3	10
Justice orientation	1	5	7	16	12	41
Commitment to church mission	12	12	11	22	19	76
Sense of humor	2	.6	2	6	20	31
Other	.6	.3	.9	.6	.3	3

In 1966 a set of qualifications extracted from interviews with formation personnel and administrators, was presented for choice. In 1982, administrators were asked to rank those same qualifications by selecting their five highest choices. Only five of the twelve characteristics were chosen by a significant number in 1982. The highest score goes to "understanding human psychology"; second rank, to "knowledge of theology." "Commitment to the mission of the church" is third; "rooted in the tradition of the congregation," fourth; and "a justice orientation and experience," fifth. These are the stand-ings, if one sums all the choices for the first five ranks for all twelve options, with write-in categories summed as "other." But, if one just looked at the highest score for each rank, "theology" would be first and "sense of humor" would replace "a justice orientation" for fifth rank.

The mission-oriented items and sense of humor were not asked in 1966, but what is clear from the 1982 choices is that commitment to mission and its implementation are now qualities sought for in formation personnel, qualities our interviewing did not find expressed in 1966. The trend is still not a major factor; focus is still predomi-nantly on the psychic side, but the social side is there in 1982.

PART IV

1. Community lifestyle

We turn now to qualities of community life. Here we will examine all those items referring to lifestyle of the individual in community, including places of residence, methods of transportation, dress, names, friends, neighborhood, cloister, budgets, local decision-making, health and retirement care, and, finally, prayer and meditation arrangements.

In 1966, most sisters lived in convents, of which there were over 12,000 in the United States. They owned and operated 1,908 different central houses, including 419 mother houses, 727 houses of study, 205 vacation houses, 76 retreat centers, and 207 infirmaries or houses of retirement.

TABLE XIII
CONGREGATIONAL BUILDINGS

	1966	1982
Mother houses	248	239
Provincial houses	171	137
Pre-novitiates	224	34
Novitiates	252	103

	1966	1982
Juniorates	173	7
Other houses of study	78	34
Infirmaries	120	103
Homes for retired sisters	87	137
Retreat houses	76	137
Vacation houses	205	205
Guest houses	39	68
Residences	Not asked	855
Other	235	415
Total	1908	2474

A glance at Table XIII reveals that ownership has radically dropped for buildings wherein education of sisters takes place, while ownership is growing for places of retirement, retreats and new uses, coded here as "other." This table lays out the reality of shifting priorities due to population change, the basic factor in all social change. They show regrouping and rearranging of life patterns as they interact with the larger society, (factors that contemplative religious orders of monks and nuns do not respond to as immediately as active sisters must do).

2. Housing and transportation

The new category, "residences," no doubt includes those smaller dwellings which sisters are now purchasing as places to live when renting becomes too expensive or when ownership becomes a practical option. Along with ownership, our data reveal that where only 2,157 sisters lived in rented dwellings in 1966, today, 11,901 so live, or 10% of all sisters, compared to 1.2% in 1966. They live now in 4,275 rented units, where they lived in only 254 such places in 1966. In 1966, this was not yet a big factor but, still, significant.

TABLE XIV

LIFESTYLE: TRANSPORTATION

	1966		1982	
Cars owned	4657	2.6%	15458	13.3%
Cars leased	719	0.4%	1642	1.4%
Total	5376	3.0%	17100	14.7%

Transportation is also different today, as Table XIV shows. While in 1966 there were an average of twelve cars per congregation, owned or leased, today there are fifty. This means an increase in car ownership by congregations from 4,657 in 1966, to 15,458 in 1982. Such a shift calls for much more administrative planning and suggests diffusion of apostolates, as well as greater independence from local parish assistance.

3. Health care

Health care is now another growing responsibility for sisters. Sisters have a modal retirement age of seventy. This has not changed since 1966, even though, in the United States, formal retirement has not been planned for by sisters. The rationalization of employment by diocese, hospital, and school, and the extensive employment of the laity, with family and individual responsibilities, have made retirement age, benefits and insurance a requisite for sisters. Because, for so many centuries, sisters have managed to create support systems for themselves, this new and sudden burden has caught the Church unawares. Who is going to provide for the sisters who have always provided for themselves? Justice says that it be the system that they serve, but such provision is a fairly recent need and one not yet fully planned for, even today. This problem is being pondered. What we know about health care is presented on Table XV.

TABLE XV

HEALTH CARE OF SISTERS

	1966		1982	
	Yes	No	Yes	No
Having a mandated retirement age	2.2%	94.9%	12.6%	86.0%
Range of age of retirement:	65-75		60-79	
Mode:	69.4		70	
	Yes	No	Yes	No
Medicare registration	93.7%	1.5%	90.4%	6.1%
Medicaid registration	Not asked		21.3%	67.3%
Private health insurance	Not asked		51.2%	41.5%
Diocesan health insurance	Not asked		33.0%	53.5%
Other health insurance	Not asked		34.8%	

The information in this table can be used with other information to understand how sisters are preparing for the future, now that their health and aging needs have to be funded out of job-related sources. At the present time, only 51.2% of those sources are linked to the local church, the traditional employer of sisters. This means that in the immediate future, more of sisters' incomes have to be allocated to providing for their aging population. Such a need forces some pragmatic choices on the works that sisters do, and necessitates an assured and growing income.

4. *Budget*

Unlike religious congregations of men, most sister groups, until the very recent past, have taken so literally the dependence factor in the vow of poverty that individual sisters, except those in very specific roles, handled no personal budget at all. In 1966, just 3.6% had introduced personal and local community budgets; but, by 1982, 89% of all congregations had made major changes in the direction of having personal budgets. This is a step not only toward personal autonomy, but also toward the need of an assured and growing income.

TABLE XVI
LIFESTYLE: RESIDENTIAL LIFE

	1966 Changes already made	1982 Changes defined as major
Horarium	71.9%	78.4%
Silence	43.6%	87.1%
Recreation	58.4%	85.4%
Chapter of faults	44.6%	93.0%
Outside activity	70.2%	76.9%
Neighborhood organization	20.6%	55.6%
Open house	12.8%	72.8%
Encourage friends	32.7%	79.2%
Personal/community budgets	3.6%	88.9%
Community decision-making	28.6%	83.9%
Other	9.0%	12.9%

5. Custom changes

Table XVI displays a set of custom changes that touch the whole order of the residential life of sisters. Prior to Vatican II, the order of the day had become quite conventionalized in convents of sisters and modeled on the cloistered contemplative life of nuns to such a degree that the works that sisters did were perceived almost as an intrusion on what was perceived as a holier dimension of their existence. This was not true for all congregations, and many people worried about it even before the Council (Neal, 1984). But the invitation to renew made it possible to put into practice the proposal made by St. Vincent de Paul in 1734. This proposal suggested that the cloister be substituted for by an inner discipline, and that the sisters free themselves from dysfunctional regulation to be more able to respond effectively to their call to mission.

Whether or not that is what the changes have provided for is a topic for another report.[7] What the data provided here do is to give us basic information about the amount of change actually introduced. Already, in 1966, changes had been made by 70% of the congregations to allow for more outside activity, but only 12.8% had opened their houses to such activity, and joining neighborhood organizations was done by only 20%. By 1982, 77% had made changes toward activity outside the religious community. On another dimension of openness to others, 32.7% were encouraging friendships in 1966; 79% in 1982. Changes in forms of recreation, rules of silence, and non-use of the chapter of faults had doubled from an average of 40% to 80%. An area of major change appears to be in the use of participatory decision-making. In 1966, 28.6% had made changes in that direction and, in 1982, 84% of congregational administrators perceived those changes as major. We will see more on this point in the section on governance.

Several experiments with new ways of living in community had been introduced by 1982. In response to an open-ended question, they were described by the respondents. Our coding of their responses yielded the following table.

[7]In 1985, Orbis Books will publish further reflections on the entire Sisters' Survey.

TABLE XVII
NEW WAYS OF LIVING IN COMMUNITY

New forms of community	% mentioned in
Intercommunity living	19.6%
Other forms of mixed communities	17.6%
Living alone	13.1%
Functionally specific arrangements	4.3%

New characteristics of communities	% mentioned in
Smaller groups	27.3%
Participation in decision-making	8.9%
Residence determined by mission	8.2%
Unstructured	2.4%
Specific characteristics	1.4%

The highlights include: 20% having sisters of different congregations living together, 18% living in other forms of mixed communities, and 13%, sisters living alone, while 9% refer to community decision-making, and 8%, to different methods of choosing to become a community, and, specifically, to ways of choosing companions in any given residence.

Two other major changes are now so much a part of the lived situation of many sisters that today the former customs have already become experienced as strange even to the sisters who participated fully in them prior to 1966. The one is use of a name different from one's baptismal name, the religious name; the other, the wearing of a religious habit. In 1966, 60% had not yet considered the option of returning to baptismal names. In 1982, 69% use their own names, with another 24% having the option of doing so or not. (Six percent did not answer the question.) Regarding religious habit, only .6% had not introduced changes in the habit by 1982; 55.6% had made major changes in the religious habit; 34% were not wearing any form of habit, and another 2% were planning major dress changes in the next five years. Some 54%

require a symbol, and 25% have an optional one. Both of these changes are major identity changes.

There is still another major set of changes that are reported for community life and these are all related to prayer and meditation, central factors of religious life. Only 20% have daily liturgy all the time; another 31% sometimes. This question was not asked in 1966. Living in smaller units and the non-availability of clergy are new factors in this reality. A variety of different forms of retreats are now available and were not in 1966. These include directed, preached, privately directed, and private non-directed, as well as other unspecified forms.

What these changes suggest, in general, is a much greater variation in the daily communal life of sisters. This, in turn, relates to their newer methods of governing themselves and the place of ministry in their lives. We will turn to these two factors, after examining a unique question concerning recommended reading.

PART V

Channels for learning social issues

One of the questions of great interest in this on-going study of sisters has been the channels through which they come to know what social issues are important and what people think about these issues. In the Sisters' Survey of 1967 and its re-test, in 1980, we have asked the sisters what they actually read. In 1966 and in 1982 we asked congregational administrators what they recommend to be read; the results are shown in Tables XVIII and XVIIIa. One has only to recall that, as late as the mid-fifties, sisters were not encouraged to be alert to the political and social commentaries on world, national and local issues. Then, with the civil rights movement, the third world movement, and the growing awareness of the relationship between church and world happenings, sisters, especially in the Sister Formation movement, began a systematic reflection on the news.

TABLE XVIII
READING RECOMMENDED

	1966 % encouraging	1982 % encouraging
Bible reading	Not asked	90.48%
Professional journals	94.20%	86.80%

	1966 % encouraging	1982 % encouraging
Religious journals	94.90%	86.00%
Daily newspapers	76.00%	85.78%
News magazines	88.10%	85.40%
Diocesan newspapers	93.90%	79.50%
Spiritual books	96.90%	76.60%
News commentaries	84.30%	74.00%
Other	15.00%	18.40%

Encouraging Bible reading is high, as Table XVIII indicates. (We did not think to ask this question in 1966.) News listening and reading is high at both times, but the encouragement to read specific journals and subject matter on justice has an over 60% encouragement in 1982. Careful examination of the data reveals no bias favoring liberal to conservative journals, Catholic or secular. The two journals that take a liberal or conservative position in their title, namely, *The New Republic* and *The National Review*, are both much lower in choice than any others. Although this information is interesting, its meaning is not clear independently of other data. The next two sections on government and apostolic perspectives provide some of that related data.

TABLE XVIIIa
NEWS MEDIA RECOMMENDED

	1966		
	High	Medium	Not recommended
U.S. News and World Report	64.60%	23.00%	.50%
Newsweek	53.80%	33.70%	1.20%
Time	39.70%	42.90%	2.90%
New York Times magazine	42.10%	24.50%	2.20%
National Review	21.50%	27.80%	3.00%
New Republic	12.30%	19.40%	4.10%
Origins	Not asked	—	—
Justice issues journals	Not asked	—	—
America	81.40%	11.60%	.00%

TABLE XVIIIa (Continued)
NEWS MEDIA RECOMMENDED

	1966		
	High	Medium	Not recommended
Sojourners	Not asked	—	—
National Catholic Reporter	27.10%	49.60%	9.20%
Commonweal	55.20%	23.80%	.50%
Diocesan papers	70.70%	9.40%	.20%
Literary journals	Not asked	—	—
Other	15.00%	1.20%	.60%

	1982		
	High	Medium	Not recommended
U.S. News and World Report	62.30%	21.10%	2.00%
Newsweek	62.00%	25.10%	.90%
Time	58.20%	27.80%	1.50%
New York Times magazine	41.20%	23.10%	8.50%
National Review	15.80%	28.10%	11.10%
New Republic	3.58%	22.20%	14.60%
Origins	76.90%	5.30%	.60%
Justice issues journals	74.60%	8.80%	.60%
America	71.40%	12.30%	.60%
Sojourners	65.20%	11.10%	2.60%
National Catholic Reporter	61.40%	24.60%	1.20%
Commonweal	51.50%	19.30%	2.30%
Diocesan papers	49.98%	24.30%	2.30%
Literary journals	45.08%	26.30%	.90%
Others	34.90%	3.00%	.30%

PART VI

1. Government in religious congregations

One area in which much change has occurred in religious congregations of women in the past twenty years is in participation in decision-making at the local level, i.e., in the residence group and in the operation of ministry. These two functions, once combined in the authority of the local superior, who was often also principal of the local school or health unit, are now quite separate. In 1966, the superior of the house was also administrator of the local ministry in 80% of the situations. That was so in only 29% of local situations in 1982 and in 60% it was specifically some other arrangement. Asked both in 1966 and in 1982 how local superiors are chosen, the administrators responding to this report show a striking contrast in methods, as Table XIX exhibits.

TABLE XIX
PARTICIPATION IN GOVERNMENT AT THE LOCAL LEVEL
Selection of local superiors

	1966%			1982%		
	Always	Some	Never	Always	Some	Never
Chosen by local sisters	1.0	.5	51.1	20.2	19.3	7.0
Chosen by provincial; sisters recommended	2.2	8.5	17.7	16.7	19.9	3.8

TABLE XIX (Continued)

PARTICIPATION IN GOVERNMENT AT THE LOCAL LEVEL
Selection of local superiors

	1966%			1982%		
	Always	Some	Never	Always	Some	Never
Chosen by provincial; no reccommendation	—	—	—	.9	9.1	12.6
Appointment by general level with consultation	7.3	13.8	9.2	4.1	2.9	14.6
Appointment by general level without consultation	81.1	6.8	9.1	.9	2.6	10.4
Other	9.4	2.7	.2	7.9	4.7	.3
No local superior	Not asked			25.4	49.7	—

From this table we can see that whereas 81% of local superiors were appointed by major superiors without any consultation with the sisters at the local level in 1966, that occurs today only in .9% of the congregations questioned. From this table, we can also see that 25% of all congregations have no local superiors today and another 50% sometimes have none. That means that, in 75% of all cases, such an option is available within American sisterhoods. What method is used for choosing local superiors and other representatives was not asked in 1966, but in 1982, in 36.5% of the cases, they are elected locally. In only 8% of the cases are they appointed.

How intermediary government officers are appointed is changing also. Today, 16% are elected by the members. This was true of only 4.6% in 1966. In 15% more of the cases today, they are elected by a province chapter, and 11% are selected from nominees presented by the sisters. In only 5% of the cases are they appointed by general government without consultation. This was true of 35.6% of the cases in 1966. What these data indicate is that choice of officers by members is constantly increasing. As can be seen from Table XX, the more participative form characterizes 42% of the congregations in 1982, compared to 18% in 1966.

TABLE XX
SELECTION OF PROVINCIAL OFFICERS

	1966	(Always)	1982
Direct vote	4.6%		16.1%
Provincial chapter elects	6.5%		14.9%
Appointment by general administrator from nominees	6.8%		11.1%
Appointment by general administrator after consultation	9.9%		8.5%
Appointment by general administrator and council	35.6%		5.3%
Other	4.6%		4.4%

2. *Election of officers*

General officers have always been elected by sisters through delegated representation at the General Chapter. The only specific difference the 1982 questioning reveals is a 10% increase in discussion of candidates prior to voting and, in discussion across the whole congregation, up from 2% in 1966. There is also a 20% increase in other unspecified methods of participation, up from 5%.

Where major changes have occurred, at the General Chapter level, is in the range and content of policy decisions deliberated and the openness of the historically participative event to the ideas of the sisters. We turn to this phenomenon now. The first question then is this one: who comes to the General Chapter? Sisters did not ask this question in 1966, because they knew the prevailing answer, i.e., delegates elected by the members and made responsible for review of policy and the making of new policy while the chapter is in session. The number of delegates was determined by the number of sisters, usually one delegate for each 200 sisters, plus the ex-officio members, who included the major officers and administrators from each province, subprovince, and delegation.

Today there is a wide variation from congregation to congregation in the changing membership at General Chapter.

TABLE XXI
PARTICIPATION IN GENERAL CHAPTER IN 1982

	Election	Appt	Exoff	Own choice
		(Unit means)		
Participation by:				
Total province membership	7.5	.1	1.9	9.8
Superiors only	.1	.01	.6	0
Sisters in final vows	3.2	.01	.6	1.5
Sisters in temporary vows	.03	0	0	.04
Outsiders	0	.003	0	.02
Others	.1	.01	.003	.13

We have no comparative data for 1966, but what characterizes chapters in 1982 is the mean number of sisters who attend by choice. This category did not exist in 1966 and is the highest number today. It indicates the new openness of the General Chapter to observers and other participants. The largest group who come in this category are sisters in perpetual vows, a mean of 1.5 per congregation.[8] Outsiders probably include consultants, members of the local church, and others invited to help the delegates deliberate the issues before them. The General

---

[8]Table XXI is made up of several independent responses. See Items 73 through 79 in the 1982 questionnaire in Appendix II.

Chapter is no longer intended only to elect general officers, leaving to them the shaping of congregational policy. That observation leads us now to examine how the ideas of the sisters get to the chapter and what the agenda is that now comes to the chapter for deliberation.

3. *Representation of points of view*

Asked in both 1966 and in 1982 how sisters represent their views to the administration, the highest percent in 1966 is "by letter to the administration," 52%, and the second highest choice is "no planned method," 34%. In 1982, the highest choice is "by assembly," 78%, a category not included in 1966 because no one had mentioned it in preparatory interviews. "Forums" is the second highest choice in 1982, 43%, again a category not offered in 1966. "No planned method" is used by only 13.7% of the 1982 group.

TABLE XXII
PREPARING AGENDA FOR GENERAL CHAPTER

(Sum of "most usual" and "quite usual")	1966	1982
By letter to administration	52.3%	42.9%
By letter from local group to administration	7.7%	16.1%
Ad hoc committees	12.9%	36.5%
Standing committees for policy	9.2%	31.3%
No planned method	34.4%	13.7%
Assemblies	Not asked	78.1%
Forums	Not asked	43.2%
Other	24.9%	32.2%

Although a range of questions were asked regarding how sisters proceed to present their proposals for agenda to the General Chapter, the responses indicate that a variety of ways was used both in 1966 and 1982. The only real difference is that the variety is greater in 1982, up from 53% to 74%, whereas in 1966 another 30% say clearly that proposals are simply submitted to the chapter committee.

4. Preparation for the General Chapter

Canonically, the General Chapter is the highest decision-making body in the congregation. This has been the case for many centuries. What is different today from the past few hundred years is the reclamation by the membership of responsibility to plan the policies that affect their lives. What is new is the focus of those policies on ministry questions that have a global justice component. This new emphasis, beginning in 1966, seems to be clearly a result of the decisions of the Second Vatican Council and of Church social teachings developing since 1891. (See O'Brien and Shannon, 1977.) Mainly, the new directions incorporate a way of speaking about ministry more expressive of the mandate of doing justice work with God's assistance than of a spirituality of withdrawal from a sinful and dangerous world. Some of this focus is seen in the change in chapter planning procedures. Asked in 1966 in an open-ended question what preparations were being made for the next chapter, the respondents took up the themes of internal procedures as seen in Table XXIII.

TABLE XXIII
PLANNED PREPARATIONS FOR CHAPTER IN 1966

	Now doing/ Have done	Plan to do
Scheduled discussions in local communities	40.2%	26.2%
Intrahouse dialogue	37.3%	18.4%

Committee work on religious life structures	36.6%	31.2%
Interhouse dialogue	36.1%	21.3%
General letter seeking suggestions from congregation	33.0%	23.2%
Theological and scriptural study	30.3%	21.5%
Study of canon law	24.0%	18.6%
Surveys	23.0%	23.5%

When asked in 1982 what characteristics were expected of the next chapter, the answers were more pastoral and social, as shown in Table XXIV.

TABLE XXIV
EXPECTED CHARACTERISTICS OF NEXT CHAPTER, 1982

	Plan to do	Plan not to do	No plan
Orientation sessions, study days, consultants	66.4%	2.9%	9.6%
Focus more on social justice	60.2%	2.6%	16.4%
Sessions open to observers	56.1%	8.5%	11.4%
Preceded by retreat days	52.0%	6.4%	20.2%
More members present as delegates	28.9%	25.4%	17.0%
One week duration	28.9%	25.1%	22.5%
Representatives of people we serve	15.5%	16.7%	43.6%
Other	24.9%	.3%	0%

With a new emphasis on mission, 60% of those responding indicated the focus of the chapter would be more on social justice. The major procedure idea was not focused on preparation before coming to the chapter but on what would be done once the delegates assembled, namely, spending time in study days and with consultants, 66%; opening the sessions to observers, 56%; and having preceding days of retreat, 52%.

Clearly, the idea of what happens at chapter has changed, as congregational administrators are well aware. One question posed in both years asked if the preparation for the next chapter would be different from that of earlier years. The response of "a great deal" was

59% in 1966 and 74% in 1982. A change then, begun in 1966, was accelerated in 1982. On the question of whether representation would be the same as before Vatican Council II, the 1966 response of "no" was 29%; it was "no" for 71% in 1982.

5. General Chapter agenda

We now come to the question of what was the agenda actually addressed in the most recent chapter. Table XXV lists these items:

TABLE XXV

AGENDA OF LAST GENERAL CHAPTER (1982 Data)

	Major issue	No issue at all
Quality of community life	69.0%	3.5%
Corporate mission	63.2%	5.8%
Simple lifestyle	56.4%	4.4%
Justice agenda of the church	49.4%	7.3%
New direction in ministry	44.7%	7.6%
Choice of ministry	35.4%	10.8%
Membership trends	30.4%	13.2%
Constitutions (write in)	21.3%	0%
Spiritual direction	20.2%	28.4%
Declining finances	17.3%	26.0%
Ownership of property	15.8%	30.4%
Pastoral ministry for women	15.8%	24.9%
Congregational stand on disarmament	15.5%	42.1%
Divestment	9.9%	37.1%
Health programs	9.4%	33.3%
Racism in workplace	7.3%	43.9%
Cost of housing	7.0%	43.0%
Retreat programs	5.8%	38.6%
Chemical dependency programs	2.0%	51.5%
Uses of testing services	1.5%	52.6%
Other	31.9%	0%

The items are arranged in descending order of importance as major issues. Sixty-nine percent found the "quality of community life" the most important issue, followed by "corporate mission," 63%; "simple lifestyle," 56%; and "justice agenda of the church," 49%; "new direction of ministry," 44.7% and "choice of ministry," 35%. On examination, it is clear that community and mission were the major concerns of the most recent chapters. The worrisome problems of declining membership, finances, ownership of property, health programs, and cost of housing were not yet explicit concerns nor were vital social issues such as "congregational stand on disarmament," "divestment," and "racism in the workplace." For many, what there was consensus on was a corporate orientation to the social mission of the church and experimentation with a communal style to implement it. The specific problems of life and ministry were, at the last chapter, still special interest group agenda.

PART VII

1. Looking to the future: expectations for the next ten years

At the end of both congregational surveys, administrators were asked to look into the future and indicate which of a selected number of outcomes they expected to happen. Ample room was left for others to be added. The listed issues were derived from the *Decree on Renewal of Religious Life* and the signs of the times back in 1966. They were repeated exactly in the 1982 survey.

TABLE XXVI
EXPECTATIONS FOR THE NEXT TEN YEARS

	1966	1982
Greater voice of sisters in planning	87.4%	88.6%
More involvement in civil/national programs	62.0%	67.8%
More involvement in public protests	14.5%	58.2%
Basic changes in style of religious life	38.0%	54.7%
Basic changes in educational work	37.5%	53.2%
Continuation of essentially the same work	63.9%	46.2%
Basic changes in welfare work	26.4%	42.7%

	1966	1982
Basic changes in health work	23.0%	40.1%
Vocation increases	31.2%	33.0%
Expansion of foundations	26.2%	13.5%
Other	1.0%	14.1%
None of these	.2%	.9%

Table XXVI reports the difference between expectations in 1966 and 1982. These categories, of course, were generated in 1966. It is of great interest that "a greater voice for sisters in planning" was the highest expectation at both the earlier and later date, with only 1% change in percentage points, 87.4% and 88.6% respectively. So too with expectation of "more involvement in civic and national programs." It is up from 62% to 68%. There is a rise of 44% in expecting involvement in public protest, a decisive shift upward in 1982. As the table records, there is a 16% increase in expectation that there will be changes in educational work, in welfare work, and health work, as well as a decline in expectation that sisters will be doing essentially the same work (63.9% to 46.2%). Ten years from then and now, only one third in each year expected and expect now vocation increases, and expectation for foundation expansion declines from 26% to 13%.

2. *Perceived most pressing needs of the world today*

With their expectations of changes in mind, what do administrators perceive to be the most pressing needs? Table XXVII deals with this.

TABLE XXVII
PERCEIVED MOST PRESSING NEEDS IN THE WORLD TODAY

	1966	1982
Relevancy of gospel to times	66.8%	81.3%
Action on behalf of the oppressed	Not asked	62.6%
Social justice	Not asked	60.2%
Open channels of communication	50.1%	55.0%
Critical social analysis	Not asked	47.4%
Knowledge of spirit of founder	45.8%	37.7%
Efforts to achieve personal sanctity	68.3%	29.5%
Careful study of society	29.8%	28.1%
Study of theological developments	43.3%	26.6%
Experiments with new kinds of community life	13.1%	14.6%
Cooperation with Sacred Congregation	59.1%	11.1%
Development of new liturgical life	32.7%	10.2%
Circumspection and patience	44.1%	6.7%
Younger members appreciating the past	23.0%	2.9%
Other	Not asked	.6%

Although "relevancy of the Gospel in our times" is highest choice in both years, as Table XXVII shows, the 1982 administrators were much stronger in affirming this need, 81% over 66.8%. "Action on behalf of the oppressed" concern followed by "social justice" are the next highest choices in 1982 and, unfortunately, these choices were not formulated for use in 1966. They have a response of 63% and 60%, respectively. (A similar finding to the Sisters' Survey Re-test of 1980.) Almost the same rank is given to "open channels of communication," 50% in 1966; 55% in 1982. "Critical social analysis" comes next, affirmed by 47.4%. It was not included in 1966. We hardly knew at that time what to call the process of looking critically at social structures to determine whose interests they serve and of planning action to make those systems just. We had to await the fine formulation of Paulo Freire for this (Freire). It is strange that, along with this emphasis, fewer than one third for each of the survey years sees as a pressing need "careful study of society," and, in view of the awareness of the need for critical social analysis, there is a decline of 17% in seeing the study of theological developments as a pressing need, down to 26.6%. The fact that cooperation with the Sacred Congregation has declined as a pressing need, from a high of 59% in 1966 to a low of 11% in 1982, from the perspective of congregational administrators, calls for serious reflection. Recall that this survey preceded the "essential elements" by a year, so we can well assume that administrators were not expecting directives counter to their internal transformations even one year prior to their promulgation.[9] "Efforts to achieve personal sanctity," a pressing need in 1966 as perceived by 68%, is down to 29.5% in 1982.

3. *Perceived major determinants of change*

TABLE XXVIII

PERCEIVED MAJOR DETERMINANTS OF CHANGE

	1966	1982
Needs of the human community	Not asked	77.8%
Ideas of the sisters	34.9%	66.7%
Human rights issues	Not asked	51.8%
Original intent of founder(s)	41.4%	50.3%
Global perspective	Not asked	41.8%
Decrees of Vatican II	84.3%	38.3%
Women's issues	Not asked	20.2%
Directives of Sacred Congregation	62.0%	18.4%

[9]On May 31, 1983 a document entitled: "Essential Elements in the Church's Teaching on Religious Life as applied to Institutes Dedicated to the Works of the Apostolate," was issued by the Vatican Congregation for Religious and Secular Institutes.

In both years, we asked what were perceived as major determinants of change in the next five years, but all our categories do not correspond. As you can see from Table XXVIII, in 1982 "the needs of the human community," has moved into first place as the causal explanation for action for most administrators, 77.8%, where "ideas of Vatican II" held primal place in 1966, 84.3%. One could easily argue that the 1982 choice is the realization of the 1966 choice and that we have here a clear picture of how charismatic ideas lead to scriptural results. "The ideas of sisters" has doubled in value as a determining factor, from 34.9% to 66.7%; "human rights issues," another newly defined determinant, is affirmed by 51.8% of administrators in 1982, again a logical outcome of the application of the ideas of Vatican II. Women's issues have clearly not yet become an explanatory variable, affirmed by only 20.2% of administrators, but 50%, ten percent more than in 1966, experience the influence of the "original intent of the founders." Another decline in perception of influence toward change is "the directives of the Sacred Congregation," expected to be such by 62% in 1966 and by only 18% in 1982. A global perspective, perhaps today the most important determinant for a Catholic Church, was recognized as a determinant by 41.8% in 1982 but we did not have the vision to pose the category in 1966.

4. Perceived main problems facing religious congregations today

We come now to the last data on apostolic perspectives in our look to the future: Table XXIX. This was the very last question and it was open-ended. Here we look at what, in respondent-created categories, are perceived to be the main problems facing religious congregations today. This question was not asked in 1966. The table displays in descending order problems felt sufficiently to be verbalized. The greatest concern is with declining numbers: 55.1% place this concern first.

TABLE XXIX

MAIN PROBLEMS FACING RELIGIOUS CONGREGATIONS TODAY

Declining numbers	55.1%
Large number of elderly	45.1%
Finances	21.1%
Effective faith development	12.1%
Discernment regarding ministry	11.4%
Responding to changing society	11.4%
Effective doing of social justice	9.9%
Need for ordination of women	1.8%
Peace-related works	1.2%

The large number of elderly sisters comes next as the concern of 45%, followed by "finances" reported by 21%. "Effective faith development" is named by 12% as a problem; and "discernment regarding ministry," by 11%; "responding to a changing society" and the "effective doing of the social justice ministry" is named by only 11% and 10%, respectively. Whether one interprets these responses to mean "only these things worry us and we can handle all other problems" or "this many of us have problems with these dimensions of ministry," those listed are real problems today.

Where is all this information to be used? The main place in 1984 is in the revision of the constitutions. For 54% of the religious congregations in the United States, the modal year for revision and submission for Church approval is 1984; 42% have already taken this step in 1982 and, for them, the modal year for such action was 1981. According to those responding to this survey, the years of greatest changes made by chapter decision were 1968-1969; 1974; and 1981. In 1982, 39% perceived their major changes to be still ahead of them. The modal year for their making them would be 1982 itself.

PART VIII

A profile of participating congregations

The three hundred forty-two different congregations and provinces which responded to this survey are equally divided among those organized into provinces, 49%, and those without provinces, 51%. Only 12.3% are diocesan congregations; 87.4% are pontifical. The average number of provinces is 1.6 in the United States; 5.1 in the world. Each congregation works in an average of 7.8 states and 2.8 countries. The states with the largest number of sisters in descending order are: California, New York, Illinois, Massachusetts, Ohio, Pennsylvania, Missouri, Texas, Florida, Maryland, Washington, D.C., Arizona and New Jersey. There is no state that has no sisters from these congregations, and they also work in fifty-seven different foreign countries. The main countries are Italy, Canada, Peru, Brazil and Mexico. France, Italy, Ireland, Germany, and French Canada are the main countries of foundation, however. Most of these congregations were founded in the early eighteen hundreds. The modal year is 1831, the earliest 480, the latest 1975. The central house for most is in the United States, for foreign locations, Rome. (See Appendix I, Table XXX for full profile.)

69

PART IX

1. Conclusions and projections

These data show clearly that major changes have occurred in all facets of the life of religious congregations of Catholic women in the United States since 1950. What has caused these changes cannot be determined by looking only at sisters, only at the Church, or only at religious causes. A complex set of factors are interwoven in this phenomenon and many of these are linked not in a chain of cause and effect but have influenced each other in interactive ways. Here I will suggest only some of the factors that are revealed in these data as they, in turn, are related to the longitudinal study of the sisters through the past twenty years. I will state my conclusions as hypotheses for further testing.

2. Hypotheses about why fewer people are entering religious life today

The first set of hypotheses focus on declining membership:

(1) The decline is directly related to wider Church

Why fewer people are entering religious life today 71

decisions and societal changes. One of these is the loss or
decline of diocesan support for city schools, when public
monies did not become available and operating costs had
significantly risen. Earlier research led to that pragmatic
decision which was made around 1968 by most dioceses.
This change, however, made the decision to keep schools
open a function of the ability of the local community to
pay for education. This decision excluded the very poor
and the not so poor and caught the schools in the
segregation-integration crisis of the inner city. Those
schools remaining open came, in time, to be diocesan
schools, thus reducing the influence of the charism of any
specific religious congregations. This eclecticism does not
provide the visibility needed for vocations to any particular group and the strife of the city is easily associated with
the administration of the school. This strife does not
inspire vocations among the city minority peoples. When
the mission to the city is more fully realized, vocations
there will have an opportunity to revive.

(2) The provision of Medicare and Medicaid for health
care, although a major advance in the provision of
human services from the Commonwealth, had the unfor-
tunate unintended result of turning private hospitals into
private enterprise systems, rendering a human service
competitive and, hence, less commitment-oriented, again
a disenchanted, pragmatic turn from an altruistic calling.

(3) The movement of Asians, Africans, and Latin
Americans into the central city reduced the religious
commitment of ethnic parishes to parish services. As the
old European ethnic Catholic members themselves prepared for their own movement to the suburbs in the early
60's, they took their churches with them, leaving the
central city unserviced by standard institutions in time of

racial strife. The witness of altruism was lacking as a stimulus to the religious calling, as the church became more a part of the establishment than of immigrant struggle. We spoke then of the suburban captivity of the churches. A racially homogeneous religious congregation doing ministries in a racially mixed community is not the best witness for vocation to a growing Third World society and Church.

(4) We should have expected some normal decline in vocations to traditional service congregations following the changes in the Church which opened up ministries to the laity in the 60's. This was a normal extension of Church life and ministry. But we should have expected also, with the new direction of ministry from Vatican II, with its emphasis on the justice agenda of eliminating the causes of poverty in contrast to only alleviating its results, that religious, called as we are to the new frontiers of ministry, would be faced with some radically new problems related to our calling. The evidence of this research indicates we have been struggling for twenty years with the needed transitions and that they are still in process.

(5) The decisions congregations made in raising the age of entering candidates from high school to some college and/or work experience broke the link of direct contact for recruitment. Young women with these backgrounds come into much less regular contact with sisters in their daily lives, and are now exposed to more options in the doing of the mission. Many groups did not provide for this change in their way of recruiting vocations.

(6) There was a reluctance in the local Church to adopt the new mission of the Church after Vatican II. "The Gathering Storm in the Churches," when some clergy and religious adopted the social gospel and others did not,

provided a witness of confusion for which a pastoral response is only now being developed.

(7) The high cost of educating new sisters to the range of professions called for by the new mission made groups experiencing new expenses reluctant to respond as spontaneously as earlier to those interested in entering but who lacked basic educational skills and needed liberal arts and professional training. Religious congregations responded well to the callings of the young professionals who joined them, but many who feel called do not have those credentials.

(8) The failure to expect recruits from the new peoples of the city is a factor in declining vocations. Religious vocations have always come from the working poor in religious congregations of sisters, as distinct from those of nuns. That is a very important point.

(9) With the decline of sisters in teaching and nursing, the probability of young women's coming in contact with sisters doing ministry gradually decreased.

(10) The slow transition in formation programs to incorporate effective programs for following the new direction of the Church's mission after the Second Vatican Council, a mission which made operative a special option for the poor,[10] rendered internal commitment to mission less visible. Some old European ethnics still define themselves as poor, even after the group to which they belong have become the new nonpoor. They continue to expect the same traditional services from sisters as they received in the past, even though it is now their turn to give rather than receive.

---

[10]The term "Special option for the poor" appears frequently in the statements of Church mission since the Second Vatican Council referring in general to the new direction of Church misison. See Donal Dorr, 1983.

(11) The severance of the link of the Catholic college from congregational formation made it very difficult for religious congregations of women to cover the costs of educating their women. Furthermore, the Catholic colleges need the sisters to link them to the prophetic ministry in the Church.

3. Some reflections on who is entering religious life today

Who is entering now? In congregations open to change, people join who see the mission in process, especially in Third World countries. If the congregation joined, however, is not able to demonstrate a formation program preparing for the doing of this mission, witnessed in practice, new members do not stay.

Other people entering include deeply committed professionals who provide human services and are seeking a community of prayer and support to reinforce this commitment which they now experience as needing God's presence.

Other people who work with sisters, hearing the sisters' new statements of mission, recognize them as the very words they have been trying to formulate as a guide for their own lives. These people, who are aware of education, nursing, community organization and other ministries, see that such ministry has a new potential when done with the new orientation of Church commitment to the poor, and they want to share the development in this new direction. They see themselves as peers working with those already committed rather than as novices being formed to an already existent program of life and work.

New members also include people who are disenchanted with the competitive struggle of modern living. Nevertheless, they want to be of service in a religious calling.

4. Reflections on ministry

Prior to the Second Vatican Council, evangelization and conscientization were seen as two different functions by most people in religious congregations. What the relationship is between "the liberation of peoples from every form of injustice and oppression" and "bringing the gospel to all facets of life by entering into the mystery of Christ" is the primary object today of theological reflection. But this is a new agenda because we have become a global community and we are a catholic church. The challenge of this agenda is the mission the apostolic congregations are choosing in their statements of mission. How to do it and how to incorporate it effectively into their Constitutions, community life, prayer and ministry is now in the process of practice and development. Because it is world changing, challenging, risk-oriented and tradition-breaking, it is approached with the range of responses we see here. The main areas of tension include: the statement of mission; formation for mission; choice of ministries; prayer and meditation forms and times; community life styles; modes of participation in decision-making; authority and responsibility; administration and accountability and, finally, the calling itself within the distinct charism of each religious congregation.

5. *A final reflection with a point of view*

There is a curious contradiction that becomes evident as we examine these pragmatic data concerning declining membership, unemployment of sisters, high costs of housing and transportation, health care, and professional education, on the one hand, and on the other, acknowledge the challenge of the new calls to the mission of assisting the poor to claim their rightful share of these very same resources that have become scarce for us, namely, membership, jobs, health care, housing and education. We have become aware of the mysterious call to obedience to God's will, in imitation of Jesus, by the witness of a simple lifestyle and the generous sharing of material resources with the oppressed poor. We have noted the freely accepted choice to forego sexual partners in order to be lovingly available to the other in need and to help build communities of people free to develop their God-given potential to be truly human, and thereby, somehow, in imitation of Jesus, to institutionalize altruism in a world that invites such a process both in secular and sacred models. It might seem that as we have moved with the church to this new mission embodying a special option for the poor, we have lost the security that others envied in our lives: the contemplative serenity, a dependable community, care in retirement, and something important and significant to do, i.e., relevant work. Yet, in reality, all these advantages have been heightened, not lost as we have responded in new ways to the mission of Jesus.

At the present time, the institutional church is finding itself challenged in its official stance as it aligns itself with the liberation struggles, such as those in Central America, where people are organizing to claim their rights to the land and to resist militarily imposed oppression. The church has become a challenge to the State when it challenges the State's stand on justice. This is a new era in the life of the church, one in which our search has brought us perhaps to an ambiguity in knowing who God is, but to more clarity as to where God is, that is, with the poor as they seek to organize in solidarity to claim their human rights and socio-economic prerogatives. The call to do God's will brings some of our traditional customs into question. How we dress, where we live, when we worship, and how we pray become problems of new concern, subordinate to the mission in which we are called to participate in a radically new way. Like many other people, sisters long for peace and joyous community, but like a much smaller number of people, they also long to do God's will, manifested to them in the Bible, in the Church, and in the signs of the times. It is in the Church and in the signs of the times that new priorities have become manifest. In a world of adequate resources but inadequate use of them, their mission to the poor has very different demands from those it had in a world of manifestly scarce resources and too many people. War no longer appears as an acceptable option for the solution of over-population, now that preference for it as such a solution has been raised to full conscience and rejected as such.

Although critical social action becomes a manifest need, preference for traditional skills is still manifest in our choice of training for mission, if not in our choice of ministry itself. /Transitions require time, reflection, prayer, choice, and planning.

What we have learned reluctantly is that shared responsibility does not obtain without shared authority,
and we have been mandated to share responsibility by
those who manage our affairs. By asking our administrators to be accountable for choices made, we have become
aware of how very difficult altruistic choice is for us when
we have power. But we are learning about the roots of
conflict and, with that, valuing more highly the making of
community. As community makers, we are learning the
essentials of dialogue but we are also learning how rare a
skill that is when command can supersede consensus. We
do not yet have evidence that we really are inventing new
models for effective action to change oppressive realities,
but we do know that trying to do so is an essential part of
our mission.

Congregations with diverse charisms are dividing up
the diverse tasks that need to be done and finding cooperation a powerful mechanism for effective action, but this
has scarcely begun. Models of caring and responsible
acting have long been a women's agenda, but how such
agenda can fit into a changing world and continue the
mission of Jesus is still a dilemma.

The data gathered here shows where changes have been
made, what choices dominate and what problems
emerge. Effective use of these data are part of the promise
of what is to come.

That God calls women to religious life we recognize as
a reality and that life is made holy by means of the vows
which express in a starkly clear way the evangelical coun-
cils, we are certain. Community life and corporate commitment to mission are highly valued. Personal and
communal prayer and asceticism we do affirm. Public
witness has shifted from that of physical appearance to

stance on social issues. Fostering a specific relationship with the church as people of God is a constant part of our new efforts toward making community, and the experience has confirmed the need of life-long formation. A form of government calling for religious authority based on faith is affirmed in our response to a call to do God's will. Where our new insights have led us, however, is to the discovery that religious authority, that is, authority that binds us together with God's people and God's mission, is far more demanding of participation in decision-making than we ever realized before. Doing this effectively is still a mystery of the life of the Church today, one to which we bind ourselves in loving and faithful obedience. One of our clearest models is one archbishop, Oscar Romero, and four women: Maura Clark, Ita Ford, Dorothy Kazel, and Jean Donovan. All dimensions of the church are found in this fivesome and their martyred witness challenges us today. They represent one of the earliest and one of the most recent congregations of religious women, the Ursulines and the Maryknoll Sisters, and the new vocation of lay volunteer. Where our religious callings send us remains a mystery, where our Church moves us does also. In that contemplative-apostolic perspective, we are currently facing a new future.

References

Dorr, Donal. *Option for the Poor: A Hundred Years of Vatican Social Teaching.* Maryknoll, New York: Orbis Books, 1983.

Erdozain, Placido. *Archbishop Romero: martyr of Salvador.* Maryknoll, New York: Orbis Books, 1981.

Flannery, Austin, O.P. *Vatican Council II: the conciliar and post conciliar documents.* Northport, New York: Costello, 1975.

Freire, Paulo. *Pedagogy of the Oppressed.* New York: Seabury, 1972.

Muckenhirn, Mary Ellen. *The Changing Sister.* Notre Dame, Indiana: Fides, 1965.

Neal, Sister Marie Augusta, SND de Namur. "From Nuns to Sisters: three significant changes in the vowed life of Catholic women." Manuscript prepared for the Association for the Sociology of Religion twentieth year volume, 1984.

O'Brien, David J. and Thomas A. Shannon. *Renewing the Earth: Catholic Documents on Peace, Justice and Liberation.* New York: Doubleday, Image Books, 1977.

Vatican Council II. "Decree on the Adaptation and Renewal of Religious Life" (Perfectae Caritatis). Boston: St. Paul's edition, 1965.

APPENDIX I
Extended Tables

TABLE IV

REASONS FOR LEAVING — 1982
Attitudes expressed by administration

Question: What do you consider the main reasons why sisters leave your congregation: before final vows (BFV); after final vows (AFV)? (These data are calculated from responses of 342 administrators who participated in the 1982 study.)

Code	Very frequent		Frequent		Seldom		Never		No answer	
Response	BFV	AFV	BFV	AFV	BFV	AFV	BFV	AFV	BFV	AFV
No vocation	17%	7%	48%	26%	19%	29%	1%	3%	23%	44%
Weak formation	3%	3%	10%	13%	33%	31%	11%	9%	44%	44%
Prefers marriage	8%	8%	41%	44%	27%	27%	2%	1%	22%	21%
Dissatisfaction with community life	5%	10%	44%	51%	22%	15%	1%	0%	27%	24%
Interest in new apostolate	1%	1%	16%	17%	32%	36%	13%	9%	38%	36%
No personal fulfillment	8%	10%	43%	45%	21%	18%	2%	1%	26%	25%
Psychological disturbance	4%	4%	4%	20%	22%	42%	39%	2%	32%	31%
Completion of professional training	0%	1%	6%	6%	27%	28%	23%	23%	44%	43%

	Very frequent BFV	Very frequent AFV	Frequent BFV	Frequent AFV	Seldom BFV	Seldom AFV	Never BFV	Never AFV	No answer BFV	No answer AFV
No clear reason	4%	3%	17%	15%	31%	29%	8%	11%	39%	41%
New appreciation of lay role	2%	1%	18%	19%	27%	30%	11%	9%	41%	41%
Disillusioned with direction of community	1%	2%	18%	31%	36%	30%	6%	1%	39%	36%
Other	0%	3%	2%	6%	1%	4%	0%	0%	97%	87%

Summary of main reasons perceived by administrators as causal of members' leaving:

Before final vows (BFV)	**Percent BFV**
No vocation	65%
Failure to achieve personal fulfillment	51%
Preference for marriage	49%
Dissatisfaction with community life	49%

After final vows (AFV)	**Percent AFV**
Dissatisfaction with community life	61%
Failure to achieve personal fulfillment	55%
Preference for marriage	52%
No vocation	33%
Disenchantment with direction of community	33%

(a) Sisters' Survey data: population survey in '67; random sample in '80 N=135105 sisters in 1967; N=3740 sisters in 1980.

TABLE IVa

REASONS FOR LEAVING — 1966
Attitudes Expressed by Administrators

Question: What do you consider the main reasons why sisters leave your congregation: before final vows (BFV); after final vows (AFV)? (These data are calculated from responses of 423 administrators who participated in the 1966 study.)

Code	Response*									
	Very frequent BFV	Very frequent AFV	Frequent BFV	Frequent AFV	Seldom BFV	Seldom AFV	Never BFV	Never AFV	No answer BFV	No answer AFV
No vocation	17%	6%	30%	10%	18%	22%	1%	5%	34%	57%

Reason					
Weak formation	2%	9%	21%	8%	60%
	3%	10%	16%	6%	64%
Prefers marriage	5%	28%	29%	2%	36%
	3%	17%	26%	3%	50%
Dissatisfied with community life	7%	33%	21%	1%	37%
	12%	36%	14%	1%	37%
Interest in new apostolate	3%	16%	28%	5%	48%
	3%	11%	22%	6%	57%
No personal fulfillment	5%	26%	17%	2%	51%
	6%	25%	12%	2%	5%
Psychological disturbance	11%	30%	27%	1%	30%
	12%	31%	22%	0%	33%
Completion of professional training	2%	4%	14%	17%	63%
	1%	6%	12%	16%	64%
No clear reason	6%	16%	17%	4%	56%
	6%	11%	8%	7%	68%
New appreciation of lay role				Not asked in 1966	
Disillusionment with direction of community				Not asked in 1966	
Other	4%	4%	1%	0%	91%
	4%	3%	1%	—	92%

Summary of main reasons perceived by administrators as causal of members' leaving

Before final vows (BFV)	**1966**
No vocation	47%
Psychological disturbance	41%
Dissatisfaction with community life	40%
Prefers marriage	33%
No personal fulfillment	31%

After final vows (AFV)	
Dissatisfaction with community life	48%
Psychological disturbance	43%
No personal fulfillment	31%
Prefers marriage	20%
No clear reason	17%

*All these data were collected in 1966

TABLE V
THE WORKS THAT SISTERS DO (a)

Teaching	Full time Unit mean (b)		Part time Unit mean	
	1966	1982	1966	1982
Pre-school	1.58	1.10	.28	.30
Elementary	152.63	41.10	3.37	6.20
High school	47.43	17.00	3.14	2.40
Catholic college	10.48	5.90	2.00	1.30
Secular college	.09	.90	.11	.20
Nursing	1.32	.40	.65	.10
Adult education	.28	.90	.83	.50
Special education	1.78	1.60	2.97	.30
Poverty program (c)	.82	.30	10.72	.20
Other	1.38	1.50	1.59	.90
Totals	217.79	70.70	25.66	12.40
Teaching administration				
School (elem, high school)	12.44	14.00	28.03	1.30
College	6.43	1.60	10.10	.20
Nursing school	.62	.20	.21	.01
Special program	.30	.40	11.97	.04
Supervisor	1.43	.40	.45	.05
Other	Not asked	1.80	Not asked	.11
Totals	21.22	18.40	50.76	1.71
Library services				
School librarian	1.94	2.60	3.31	1.30
College librarian	.78	.70	.28	.30
Medical librarian	.92	.40	.30	.23
Other	.08	.40	.12	.40
Totals	3.72	4.10	4.01	2.23
Clerical service				
Business office	3.24	2.70	.97	.90
Secretarial work	1.35	3.10	1.22	1.40
Other	.35	.90	.28	.50
Totals	4.94	6.70	2.47	2.80

(a) These data are from the surveys of congregations of religious women sponsored by LCWR in 1966 and 1982.

(b) Unit mean is the national average number of sisters per unit (congregation or province) engaged in a particular work. An average unit in 1966 consists of 411 sisters; in 1982, 306.

(c) Migrant education plus poverty programs sponsored by government.

1966:n=423 congregations:173866 sisters included:24000 missing
1982:n=342 congregations:104538 sisters included:26000 missing

TABLE Va
THE WORKS THAT SISTERS DO

Missionary and catechetical works

	Full time Unit mean		Part time Unit mean	
	1966	1982	1966	1982
Foreign missions	6.64	4.60	.53	.05
Home missions	3.95	1.40	1.98	.10
Convert work	.00	.10	.56	.20
Retreat work	1.37	1.40	.61	.80
CCD instruction	4.37	4.80	66.23	7.40
Campus ministry	.08	.70	.35	.10
Adult catechetical	.46	.50	.44	.20
CCD teacher training	.45	1.40	2.89	.80
Catech materials development	.02	.20	.24	.20
House of prayer		.90		.30
Other	.31	7.70	1.09	1.20
Total	17.65	23.70	74.92	11.35

Health care

	Full time Unit mean		Part time Unit mean	
	1966	1982	1966	1982
Physician	.16	.30	.00	.05
Professional nurse	13.69	6.30	.76	.60
L.P.N.	1.44	1.50	.38	.20
Psychiatrist	.04	.03	.00	.00
Clinical phsychologist	.11	.20	.10	.05
Dentist	.03	.02	.01	.00
Dietician	1.10	.50	.11	.10
Pharmacist	.48	.30	.11	.10
Lab technician	1.45	.70	.14	.10
Other	1.87	5.20	.32	1.30
Total	20.37	15.05	1.93	2.50

Health administration

Hospital	2.72	1.70	.28	.10
Infirmary	.48	.50	.20	.10
Clinic	.25	.20	.06	.04
Nursing home	.54	.70	.07	.10
Other	.19	1.00	.05	.10
Total	4.18	4.10	.66	.44

Staff of national organizations

NCEA, other church	.01	.03	.06	.02
LCWR, NARW, other religious	.00	.10	.03	.10
National CCD	.03	.01	.22	.03
Formation	.03	.03	.11	.05
A publication	.01	.03	.06	.04
Other	.02	.23	.07	.03
Total	.10	.43	.55	.27

TABLE Vb

THE WORKS THAT SISTERS DO

Social service	Full time Unit mean		Part time Unit mean	
	1966	1982	1966	1982
School counseling	.56	1.10	2.81	.20
Family counseling	.07	.40	.11	.10
Social case work	.59	.70	.26	.04
Medical social work	.08	.30	.02	.10
Community organizing	.07	.50	.23	.10
Inner city programs	.26	.80	1.29	.10
Group work	.12	.20	.17	.04
Home visiting	.35	1.10	6.61	1.10
Settlement house	.16	.20	.40	.10
Maternity/Infant home	.33	.10	.01	.02
Orphanage	2.09	.40	.27	.02
Residence for working women	.40	.10	.02	.10
Guest house	.26	.10	.01	.04
Home for deliquent	.49	.20	.24	.02
Home for aged	2.87	1.60	.47	.40
Home administration	.85	.60	.09	.05
Family shelter/bat women		.20		.20
Drug abuse		.10		.04

Other	1.13	2.50	.42	.70
Total	10.68	11.20	13.43	3.47
Staff within congregation				
General administration	2.82	2.80	.79	.60
Provincial administration	2.00	2.30	.61	.70
Formation	2.15	1.20	.71	.90
Special programs	.09	.10	.24	.10
Vocation work	.34	.50	2.87	.70
Public relations	.25	.10	.42	.20
Communications	.15	.20	.72	.30
Archivist		.50		.50
Program for retired		1.50		.60
Research		.10		.10
Other	.57	1.30	.20	.60
Total	8.37	10.60	6.56	5.30
Other services				
Kitchen services	10.06	3.40	1.65	1.00
Maintenance	1.15	.70	.63	.30
Housekeeper	4.17	1.50	3.78	.80
Care of rectory etc.	1.18	.40	.06	.10
Seamstress	2.18	.50	1.48	.60
Printing, binding	.20	.10	.23	.10
Sacristan	.92	.60	6.23	1.00
Receptionist	.70	.70	1.40	1.80
Other	1.09	1.80	.87	.90
Total	21.65	9.70	16.33	6.60
Total Table V, Va, Vb	330.67	174.68	197.28	49.07

TABLE VII

PROFESSIONAL PREPARATION: 1966 and 1982

Percent of Bachelors', Masters' and Doctoral Degrees

	1982 % of B.A.	1966 % M.A.	1982	1966 % Ph.D.	1982
Economics	.2	.2	.2	.7	.7
Political Science	.2	.1	.1	.5	.5
Psychology	.9	.8	.9	4.7	5.0
Sociology	1.7	1.3	.7	2.7	2.2
Anthropology	.0	.0	.0	.7	.3
History	9.0	5.7	4.3	8.3	6.0
Total Social Sciences	12.0	8.1	6.2	17.6	14.7

French	1.5	2.5	1.7	4.0	3.5
German	.1	.1	.2	.4	.7
Italian	.0	.1	.0	.1	.1
Latin	1.7	1.4	1.3	1.7	1.4
Greek	.0	.0	.0	.0	.2
Spanish	.8	1.4	1.0	1.9	1.4
Russian	.0	.1	.0	.1	.1
Other languages	.0	.0	.0	.0	.0
Linguistics	.0	.1	.1	.4	.6
Total Language	4.1	5.7	4.3	8.6	8.0
Biology	1.6	2.0	1.6	5.6	4.0
Chemistry	1.1	1.4	1.2	4.3	5.0
Geography	.2	.2	.2	.4	.3
Mathematics	3.0	4.3	3.2	6.1	4.4
Physics	.1	.4	.3	.7	.6
Statistics	.0	.0	.0	.0	.1
Science, General	.7	1.5	.8	1.8	.2
Total Math/Science	6.7	9.8	7.3	18.9	14.6
Arts/Fine Arts	1.1	2.3	1.7	.2	1.2
Drama	.1	.6	.4	.8	.5
Music	3.3	3.5	3.0	3.2	2.1
Literature/English	13.3	9.2	6.9	14.8	11.6
Philosophy	.7	.8	.4	5.0	3.9
Total Humanities	18.5	16.4	12.4	24.0	19.3
Law	.0	.0	.1	.0	1.6
Medical Technician	.5	.2	.2	.1	.1
Nursing	5.5	2.7	2.6	.7	1.6
Medical Doctor	.1	.0	.0	2.3	4.8
Psychiatry	.0	—	.1	—	.1
Total Medical/Law	6.1	2.9	3.0	3.1	8.2
Education/Special Ed	41.9	33.5	26.1	15.6	13.2
Social Work	.5	1.1	1.9	.1	1.0
Counseling	.1	2.0	4.1	1.1	1.3
Library Science	.5	3.4	2.9	.5	.2
Administration	.3	4.3	7.7	1.7	2.9
Business	1.8	2.3	2.5	.4	.3
Home Economics	.9	1.1	.8	.6	.6
Journalism	.1	.2	.1	.1	.0
Engineering	.0	—	.0	—	.0
Communication Arts	.0	—	.3	—	.5

	B.A. 1982	M.A. 1966	M.A. 1982	Ph.D. 1966	Ph.D. 1982
Advertising	.0	—	.0	—	.0
Total Service Professions	46.2	47.9	46.4	20.1	20.0
Theology	1.5	8.6	13.9	6.3	7.5
Other	4.4	.9	6.2	1.7	7.6
Total Frequency	53391	25196	41828	1666	2924

TABLE XXX

GENERAL CHARACTERISTICS OF US CATHOLIC WOMEN'S CONGREGATIONS IN 1982

Structure (a)

Congregations with provinces in 1982	49.4%
Congregations without provinces in 1982	50.6%

Mean number of provinces in congregations with provinces

	1966	1982
In world	4.3	5.1
In United States	1.4	1.6

Type of congregation

Diocesan	12.3%
Pontifical	87.4%

Location

Mean number of countries where located	2.8
Mean number of states where located	7.8

Percent of congregations or provinces in various states of the US

State	%	State	%	State	%
Alabama	14.3	Maine	7.0	Oregon	7.9
Alaska	7.0	Maryland	24.9	Pennsylvania	27.5
Arizona	21.1	Massachusetts	30.7	Rhode Island	12.9
Arkansas	3.5	Michigan	22.8	South Carolina	7.3
California	37.4	Minnesota	18.7	South Dakota	9.1
Colorado	19.0	Mississippi	11.1	Tennessee	11.7
Connecticut	19.6	Missouri	26.3	Texas	26.0
Delaware	5.3	Montana	7.3	Utah	2.9
Florida	26.0	Nebraska	12.6	Vermont	3.8
Georgia	10.0	Nevada	3.8	Virginia	12.9
Hawaii	4.7	New Hampshire	7.3	Washington	14.3

Idaho	4.1	New Jersey	20.5	Wash, D.C.	21.6
Illinois	35.1	New Mexico	15.5	West Virginia	11.1
Indiana	19.3	New York	36.5	Wisconsin	16.7
Iowa	10.8	North Carolina	11.4	Wyoming	2.9
Kansas	7.9	North Dakota	7.6	Puerto Rico	7.0
Kentucky	13.7	Ohio	27.8		
Louisiana	17.8	Oklahoma	9.4		

Percent of congregations or provinces in other countries

Angola	.6	Haiti	1.8	Portugal	2.0
Argentina	3.2	Honduras	1.2	Scotland	1.5
Australia	2.6	India	4.1	South Africa	2.9
Belgium	5.0	Ireland	6.7	Spain	4.1
Belize	1.5	Israel	2.0	Taiwan	4.1
Bolivia	5.0	Italy	22.8	Tanzania	1.8
Brazil	14.0	Japan	8.5	Uganda	1.2
Canada	16.1	Kenya	3.2	Venezuela	2.0
Chile	5.3	Korea	2.3	Zaire	2.0
China	.9	Malawi	.6	Zimbabwe	.6
Colombia	4.4	Mexico	9.9	South East Asia	5.0
Costa Rica	.6	Mozambique	.9	Other Africa	16.4
Cuba	.3	Netherlands	1.2	Other East	
Dominican		New Zealand	1.2	Europe	2.0
Republic	.3	Nicaragua	5.3	Other Europe	3.5
Ecuador	2.0	Nigeria	2.0	Other Latin	
El Salvador	1.2	Pakistan	.6	American	5.6
England	8.2	Paraguay/Uruguay	2.3	Other Mid/East	1.5
France	7.6	Peru	14.6	(other)	15.2
Germany	5.6	Philippines	2.0		
Guatemala	4.4	Poland	1.5		

(a) 342 different congregations or provinces are represented here.

Change in province structure	1966-1982 % of total	Modal year
Newly divided into provinces	21.1	1968
Reduced number of provinces	8.5	1976
Eliminated provinces	3.8	1976

Place and time of foundation

Place	% total	Place	% total
United States	27.5	Netherlands	.6
France	26.6	Spain	.6

Italy	14.0	Poland	.6
Ireland	9.6	Other Eastern Europe	.9
Germany	7.6	Scotland	.3
French Canada	2.9	Latin America	.3
England	1.5	Africa	.3
Belgium	1.2	Other	1.5
English Canada	.6		

Time of foundation	Number of foundations founded in this time span	Modal year and number founded	
300-1000	20	480	5
1200-1600	20	1535	8
1601-1700	42	1650	23
1701-1800	19	1775	6
1801-1900	205	1831	22
1901-1975	36	1923	3

Location of motherhouses of participating congregations (a)

United States	219		
New York	22	California	7
Pennsylvania	21	Michigan	7
Ohio	16	Minnesota	7
Indiana	13	Louisiana	7
Texas	13	Maryland	6
Missouri	12	Kentucky	6
Illinois	9	Kansas	5
Massachusetts	8	Iowa	5
Wisconsin	8	New Jersey	5

Countries other than US where motherhouses of these congregations are located (a)

Italy	52
France	28
French Canada	11
Belgium	8
English Canada	5
Ireland	5

APPENDIX II
Questionnaires Used in This Research

RELIGIOUS COMMUNITY SURVEY
SPONSORED BY
THE CONFERENCE OF MAJOR RELIGIOUS
SUPERIORS OF
WOMEN'S INSTITUTES OF
THE UNITED STATES

RESEARCH DIVISION

SUMMER, 1966

PART I — TO MAJOR SUPERIORS

This questionnaire is the first part of a survey sponsored by the Conference of Major Superiors as a service to religious orders in the United States. The purpose of this section is to gather information about each religious congregation. Such information can later be used for comparative purposes in planning programs, preparing for chapters, and in general, implementing the Decree on the Appropriate Renewal of Religious Life.

Because of the importance of the survey for future use, we ask that you respond as accurately as possible, or have someone who is fully informed do it for you. We can guarantee by the method used for recording and reporting results that your anonymity will be fully assured. Both you who give the information and your congregation will remain anonymous to the degree you wish anonymity preserved.

1. CONGREGATION   This is the number which in our
   NUMBER   _____ survey refers to your congrega-
                                        tion.

2. PROVINCE OR   This is the number which in our
   AREA NUMBER   _____ survey refers to your province
                                        or area.

   N.B. Please place one of these numbers on *each page* of the
   questionnaire in the space provided. If you are a Superior General
   use your Congregation Number; if you are a Provincial Superior,
   use only your Province Number. We urge you to record and keep
   these numbers for your own future reference.

3. Are you a Superior General or a Provincial Superior?
   _____ (1 Superior General   _____(2 Provincial Superior

I. GEOGRAPHY

4. In what states of the United States and in what foreign countries
   does your order have houses?
   A. UNITED STATES

   _____(1   _____(11   _____(21
   _____(2   _____(12   _____(22
   _____(3   _____(13   _____(23
   _____(4   _____(14   _____(24
   _____(5   _____(15   _____(25
   _____(6   _____(16   _____(26
   _____(7   _____(17   _____(27
   _____(8   _____(18   _____(28
   _____(9   _____(19   _____(29
   _____(10   _____(20   _____(30

   B. FOREIGN COUNTRIES

   _____(1   _____(6   _____(11
   _____(2   _____(7   _____(12
   _____(3   _____(8   _____(13
   _____(4   _____(9   _____(14
   _____(5   _____(10   _____(15

5. Is yours a diocesan order?   _____(1 Yes   _____(2 No

If any question requires further explanation, please feel free to add comments. Make a notation in the margin if the comment is brief; if the comment is longer, write it at the *end of the questionnaire*. Just be sure to give the *number of the question* to which your comment applies. Should you have no available data for a particular question, or should data not be immediately available but could be supplied later, kindly note in the margin:

a) No data

b) Sending data later
N.B. When data is sent later, please be sure to include your Congregation or Province Number.

This questionnaire is being sent to the Superiors General and the Provincial Superiors of religious congregations in the United States who are members of the CMSW. To prevent overlapping, will you please answer in the following manner.

If you are a Superior General, kindly give information for those persons and houses under your *direct* jurisdiction, *excluding* what will be reported by your Provincial Superiors. If there is even one house or institution which does not belong to a province, please indicate it in the data you report. In case your congregation is not divided into provinces, answer for the entire order.

If you are a Provincial Superior, please answer just for *your own province*, except when the question explicitly asks about the entire congregation.

6. What was the population of your province as of June 1966?

_____(1 All sisters who have made vows
_____(2 juniors or scholastics only
_____(3 novices
_____(4 postulants
_____(5 candidates or aspirants
_____(6 total of 1 - 5

7. In what states of the United States and foreign countries do you have jurisdiction?

A. Unites States:	No. of houses:	United States:	No. of houses:
_____(1	____(1	_____(11	____(11
_____(2	____(2	_____(12	____(12
_____(3	____(3	_____(13	____(13

_____(4	_____(4	_____(14	_____(14
_____(5	_____(5	_____(15	_____(15
_____(6	_____(6	_____(16	_____(16
_____(7	_____(7	_____(17	_____(17
_____(8	_____(8	_____(18	_____(18
_____(9	_____(9	_____(19	_____(19
_____(10	_____(10	_____(20	_____(20

(if more space is required, record at end of questionnaire.)

B. Foreign Countries: No. of houses: Foreign Countries: No. of houses:

_____(1	_____(1	_____(11	_____(11
_____(2	_____(2	_____(12	_____(12
_____(3	_____(3	_____(13	_____(13
_____(4	_____(4	_____(14	_____(14
_____(5	_____(5	_____(15	_____(15
_____(6	_____(6	_____(16	_____(16
_____(7	_____(7	_____(17	_____(17
_____(8	_____(8	_____(18	_____(18
_____(9	_____(9	_____(19	_____(19
_____(10	_____(10	_____(20	_____(20

II. WORK CATEGORIES

8. Please indicate the *number* of your sisters engaged on a full-time
or part-time basis in the types of work listed below. There are
five major categories:

> A. Teaching and Educational Administration
> B. Missionary and Catechetical Work
> C. Health Care and Administration
> D. Social Service
> E. Special Staff Functions and Services

Be sure to look through all the categories before you start filling
them in. We realize that some types of work can go under several
names; what we ask is that you choose the listing which most
closely describes the work a given sister does and list her only
once for *that* work. If she works part-time in several areas, the
sister will be listed in several different categories, but only one
time for each specific type of work. Because of the part-time
listing, therefore, the numbers you give will exceed the total
number of persons within your congregation.

Should a work you do not fit under any of these categories, add it at the end of the questionnaire with the requested information.

8. A) Teaching and Educational Administration

Time Full-	Part-	Teaching in:	Time Full-	Part-	Teaching in:
__ (1	__ (1	pre-school	__ (7	__ (7	school of nursing
__ (2	__ (2	elementary	__ (8	__ (8	secular university
__ (3	__ (3	private, parochial, diocesan, high school of your sisters	__ (9	__ (9	adult education
			__ (10	__ (10	special education (e.g., retarded)
__ (4	__ (4	inter-community high school	__ (11	__ (11	poverty programs (e.g. Headstart)
__ (5	__ (5	your community college	__ (12	__ (12	migrant education
__ (6	__ (6	inter-community college	__ (13	__ (13	other: (specify) _____ _____

Time Full-	Part-	Administration:	Time Full-	Part-	Administration:
__ (1	__ (1	school	__ (4	__ (4	special program
__ (2	__ (2	college	__ (5	__ (5	supervisor
__ (3	__ (3	nursing school			

8. B) Missionary and Catechetical Work

Time Full-	Part-		Time Full-	Part-	
__ (1	__ (1	foreign missions	__ (6	__ (6	Newman centers, etc.
__ (2	__ (2	home missions	__ (7	__ (7	adult catechetical centers
__ (3	__ (3	convert work	__ (8	__ (8	CCD teacher training
__ (4	__ (4	retreat work			
__ (5	__ (5	CCD instruction for children and similar programs	__ (9	__ (9	catechetical materials development
			__ (10	__ (10	other: (specify) _____ _____

8. C) Health Care and Administration

Time Full-	Part-	Direct care as:	Time Full-	Part-	Direct care as:
__ (1	__ (1	physician	__ (6	__ (6	dentist
__ (2	__ (2	professional nurse	__ (7	__ (7	dietitian

— (3 — (3 nurse's aide   — (8 — (8 pharmacist
— (4 — (4 psychiatrist   — (9 — (9 lab. technician
— (5 — (5 clinical psychologist   — (10 — (10 other: (specify)

_____

_____

Time				Time		
Full-	Part-	Administration:		Full-	Part-	Administration:
— (1	— (1 hospital			— (4	— (4 nursing home	
— (2	— (2 infirmary			— (5	— (5 other: (specify)	
— (3	— (3 clinic					

_____

_____

8. D) Social Service

Time		Time	
Full-	Part-	Full-	Part-
— (1	— (1 school counselling	— (10	— (10 maternity-infant homes
— (2	— (2 family counselling	— (11	— (11 homes for orphans
— (3	— (3 social case work	— (12	— (12 residence for working girls
— (4	— (4 medical social work	— (13	— (13 resident or guest houses
— (5	— (5 community organizing	— (14	— (14 homes for delinquents
— (6	— (6 inner city programs (other than teaching)	— (15	— (15 homes for the aged
— (7	— (7 group work (e.g. neighborhood house director)	— (16	— (16 administration of above-mentioned homes
— (8	— (8 home visiting program	— (17	— (17 other: (specify)
— (9	— (9 neighborhood or settlement house		

_____

_____

8. E) Special Staff Functions and Services

Time			Time		
Full-	Part-	Staff within community:	Full-	Part-	
— (1	— (1 general administration		— (5	— (5 vocation work	
— (2	— (2 provincial administration		— (6	— (6 public relations	
— (3	— (3 formation programs		— (7	— (7 publications	
— (4	— (4 special programs (e.g. tertian)		— (8	— (8 other: (specify)	

_____

_____

Time			Time		
Full-	Part-	On staff of national organization:	Full-	Part-	
__ (1	__ (1	NCEA	__ (4	__ (4	Sister Formation
__ (2	__ (2	CMSW	__ (5	__ (5	a publication
__ (3	__ (3	CCD	__ (6	__ (6	other: (specify)
			6		_____
					_____

Time			Time		
Full-	Part-	Library Services:	Full-	Part-	
__ (1	__ (1	school librarian	__ (4	__ (4	medical records
__ (2	__ (2	college librarian			librarian
__ (3	__ (3	medical librarian	__ (5	__ (5	other: (specify)
					_____
					_____

Time			Time		
Full-	Part-	Clerical services:	Full-	Part-	
__ (1	__ (1	business offices	__ (3	__ (3	other: (specify)
__ (2	__ (2	secretarial work			_____
					_____

Time			Time		
Full-	Part-	Domestic services: etc.	Full-	Part-	
__ (1	__ (1	kitchen service	__ (6	__ (6	printing, binding
__ (2	__ (2	maintenance	__ (7	__ (7	altar preparations
__ (3	__ (3	housekeeper	__ (8	__ (8	receptionist
__ (4	__ (4	care of rectories, seminaries, etc.	__ (9	__ (9	other: (specify)
__ (5	__ (5	seamstress			_____
					_____

(Do not include ordinary housework every sister may do regularly.)

III. INSTITUTIONS

9. Please give the number for your province (or congregation if no provinces) of separate institutions staffed by your sisters and which fall into the following categories:

Institution	community owned	diocesan owned	parish owned	other:	(specify)
1) pre-school	____ (1	____ (1	____ (1	____ (1	_____
2) elementary	____ (2	____ (2	____ (2	____ (2	_____

3) high school   _____ (3 _____ (3 _____ (3 _____ (3 _____
4) junior college   _____ (4 _____ (4 _____ (4 _____ (4 _____
5) college   _____ (5 _____ (5 _____ (5 _____ (5 _____
6) graduate school _____ (6 _____ (6 _____ (6 _____ (6 _____
7) nursing school   _____ (7 _____ (7 _____ (7 _____ (7 _____
8) special school   _____ (8 _____ (8 _____ (8 _____ (8 _____
9) religious center _____ (9 _____ (9 _____ (9 _____ (9 _____
10) retreat house   _____ (10 _____ (10 _____ (10 _____ (10 _____
11) hospital   _____ (11 _____ (11 _____ (11 _____ (11 _____
12) clinic   _____ (12 _____ (12 _____ (12 _____ (12 _____
13) nursing home   _____ (13 _____ (13 _____ (13 _____ (13 _____
14) social welfare
    center   _____ (14 _____ (14 _____ (14 _____ (14 _____
15) maternity-infant
    home   _____ (15 _____ (15 _____ (15 _____ (15 _____
16) child care center _____ (16 _____ (16 _____ (16 _____ (16 _____
17) home for
    orphans   _____ (17 _____ (17 _____ (17 _____ (17 _____
18) home for
    delinquents   _____ (18 _____ (18 _____ (18 _____ (18 _____
19) home for
    working girls   _____ (19 _____ (19 _____ (19 _____ (19 _____
20) home for aged   _____ (20 _____ (20 _____ (20 _____ (20 _____
21) guest house   _____ (21 _____ (21 _____ (21 _____ (21 _____
22) other: (specify) _____ (22 _____ (22 _____ (22 _____ (22 _____

_____ _____ _____ _____ _____ _____
_____ _____ _____ _____ _____ _____

10. Please indicate the number of community buildings which are under your jurisdiction.

Community Buildings:

_____ (1 mother house   _____ (8 infirmary
_____ (2 provincial house   _____ (9 home for retired sisters
_____ (3 aspirancy   _____ (10 retreat house
_____ (4 postulate   _____ (11 vacation house
_____ (5 novitiate   _____ (12 guest house
_____ (6 juniorate   _____ (13 other: (specify)
_____ (7 other houses of study

                               _____
                               _____

IV. TREND DATA

In order to find out what trends are common to many religious orders we need to have a clear picture of admissions and withdrawals during the years of changing patterns since World War II.

11. Please indicate whether the following information is for a province or a whole congregation. Check one.

_____(1 province   _____(2 congregation

12. How many girls entered religious life in your province (or congregation, if you are responding for an order with no provinces) in each of the following periods?

	No. entered	No. of these who made first vows	No. of these who made perpetual vows	No. of these who are still in the congregation
1) 1948 - 1952	_____ (1	_____ (1	_____ (1	_____ (1
2) 1953 - 1957	_____ (2	_____ (2	_____ (2	_____ (2
3) 1958 - 1962	_____ (3	_____ (3	_____ (3	_____ (3
4) 1963 - 1965	_____ (4	_____ (4	_____ (4	_____ (4

13. How many of the following kinds of buildings have come under your management during the years:

Part A

	Years 1951 - 1955	Years 1956 - 1960	Years 1961 to 1965
1) novitiate house	_____ (1	_____ (1	_____ (1
2) house of study	_____ (2	_____ (2	_____ (2
3) provincial house	_____ (3	_____ (3	_____ (3
4) postulate	_____ (4	_____ (4	_____ (4
5) infirmary	_____ (5	_____ (5	_____ (5
6) vacation house	_____ (6	_____ (6	_____ (6

Part B

	Community-owned 1951 to 1955	1956 to 1960	1961 to 1965	Not Community-owned 1951 to 1955	1956 to 1960	1961 to 1965
1) elementary school	__ (1	__ (1	__ (1	__ (1	__ (1	__ (1
2) high school	__ (2	__ (2	__ (2	__ (2	__ (2	__ (2
3) junior college	__ (3	__ (3	__ (3	__ (3	__ (3	__ (3
4) college	__ (4	__ (4	__ (4	__ (4	__ (4	__ (4
5) hospital	__ (5	__ (5	__ (5	__ (5	__ (5	__ (5
6) orphanage	__ (6	__ (6	__ (6	__ (6	__ (6	__ (6
7) other: (specify)						
_____	__ (7	__ (7	__ (7	__ (7	__ (7	__ (7
_____	__	__	__	__	__	__

14. Please indicate where changes in foundations took place in your province (or order, if no provinces) from:

	1956 - 1960			1961 - 1965		
	No. in central city	No. in suburbs	No. in rural areas	No. in central city	No. in suburbs	No. in rural areas
1) houses opened or works undertaken	___ (1	___ (1	___ (1	___ (1	___ (1	___ (1
2) houses closed or works abandoned	___ (2	___ (2	___ (2	___ (2	___ (2	___ (2

15. Do you have a specific retirement age? _____(1 yes _____(2 no

16. If yes, what is it? _____

17. When did you introduce it? Year _____

18. Are your eligible sisters registered for the Medicare Program?
        _____(1 yes   _____(2 no

19. Did you have an insurance plan for health care prior to Medicare?
              _____(1 yes   _____(2 no

20. How many sisters do you have over 65 in your province (or order, if no provinces)?
    _____ No. over 65

21. How many sisters are inactive due to ill health or old age?

	ill health	old age
1) inactive	_____ (1	_____ (1
2) partially inactive, but still engaged in part-time work in the community, (e.g. tutoring small groups, working in the house, etc.)	_____ (2	_____ (2

V. SCREENING PROCEDURES

22. Because of the variety of results from experimentation with testing programs, we wish to gather the available information on what has been tried. Kindly check those spaces which apply in your case.
        _____ (1 We have never had a testing program prior to admissions and are not planning to have one.

——————— (2 We are planning such a program
——————— (3 We are just beginning our first program now.
——————— (4 We had a program but have discontinued it.
——————— (5 We have a program and expect to continue it.
——————— (6 We have a program and are planning to discontinue it.
——————— (7 We have a program and are reevaluating it.
——————— (8 other: (specify)

———————————————————————
———————————————————————

23. If you had a testing program but have discontinued it, how long did you have it and when did you discontinue it?

————(a number of years ————————(b date program was terminated

24. Why did you discontinue it? ———————————————————
——

25. Which of the following types of tests are given to candidates applying to your congregation? Are they given to all candidates or just selected candidates? For how long have you used these tests? Please check as many categories as apply.

Type of Test	Candidates who are tested			No. of years used
	All	Most	Few	
— (1 IQ	—— (1	—— (2	—— (3	—— (1
— (2 Vocational Inventory	—— (1	—— (2	—— (3	—— (2
— (3 Standard Personality Test	—— (1	—— (2	—— (3	—— (3
— (4 Projective Test	—— (1	—— (2	—— (3	—— (4
— (5 College Entrance Examination	—— (1		—— (3	—— (5
— (6 other: (specify)				
————————	—— (1	—— (2	—— (3	—— (6
————————	——	——	——	——

26. Please record here the code number beside the tests listed above for those tests you have found most useful and those least useful.

Most Useful	Least Useful
————————(1	————————(1
————————(2	————————(2
————————(3	————————(3

27. Which of the following types of interviews are given to candidates applying to your congregation? Please check as many categories as apply.

Interviews	Candidates who are interviewed			No. of years used
	All	Most	Few	
__ (1 Interview with Sister trained in Psychology	____ (1	____ (2	____ (3	____ (1
__ (2 Interview with Mistress	____ (1	____ (2	____ (3	____ (2
__ (3 Interview with Provincial Superior	____ (1	____ (2	____ (3	____ (3
__ (4 Interview with vocation director	____ (1	____ (2	____ (3	____ (4
__ (5 Interview with local superior	____ (1	____ (2	____ (3	____ (5
__ (6 other: (specify) _____ _____	____ (1	____ (2	____ (3	____ (6

28. Please record here the code number beside the interviews listed above for those interviews you have found most useful and those least useful.

Most Useful	Least Useful
_____ (1	_____ (1
_____ (2	_____ (2
_____ (3	_____ (3

29. Which of the following types of credentials are requested from candidates applying to your congregation? Please check as many categories as apply.

Credentials	Candidates who are requested			No. of years used
	All	Most	Few	
__ (1 Recommendation from pastor	____ (1	____ (2	____ (3	____ (1
__ (2 Recommendation from sister in community	____ (1	____ (2	____ (3	____ (2
__ (3 Letter from someone who knows the family	____ (1	____ (2	____ (3	____ (3

— (4 Letter from business ____ (1 ____ (2 ____ (3 ____ (4
acquaintance of
family
— (5 Letters from teachers ____ (1 ____ (2 ____ (3 ____ (5
— (6 other: (specify)

_____ ____ (1 ____ (2 ____ (3 ____ (6

30. Please record here the code number beside the types of credentials listed above for those types of credentials you have found most useful and those least useful.

Most Useful | Least Useful
____(1 | ____(1
____(2 | ____(2
____(3 | ____(3

31. If you have made substantial changes in your testing program in the past two years, please state briefly reasons for the changes:

_____
_____
_____

32. If you have a testing program please indicate who administers the test and who interprets the test. Put a (1) if the person always administers or always interprets the test; put a (2) if the person sometimes administers or sometimes interprets the test. Mark as many categories as apply.

Admin-isters	Inter-prets		Admin-isters	Inter-prets	
___ (1	___ (1	lay professional psychiatrist	___ (6	___ (6	non-professional sister
___ (2	___ (2	lay professional psychologist	___ (7	___ (7	vocation director
___ (3	___ (3	sister professional psychiatrist	___ (8	___ (8	professional testing agency (e.g. CEEB service)
___ (4	___ (4	sister professional psychologist	___ (9	___ (9	inter-community arrangements
___ (5	___ (5	sister with some training in psychology	___ (10	___ (10	other: (specify)

_____
_____
_____

33. Which of the following would usually be considered reasons for not accepting candidates? Check as many as possible.

	Always	Sometimes	Never
1) Illegitimacy	_____ (1	_____ (2	_____ (3
2) Marriage vows	_____ (1	_____ (2	_____ (3
3) Intellectual level	_____ (1	_____ (2	_____ (3
4) Disrupted family background	_____ (1	_____ (2	_____ (3
5) Age	_____ (1	_____ (2	_____ (3
6) Belonging to another rite	_____ (1	_____ (2	_____ (3
7) other: (specify)			
_____	_____ (1	_____ (2	_____ (3
_____	_____	_____	_____

34. If there is a limitation in regard to intellectual level, what standards are required?

   _____

   _____

35. If there are restrictions in regard to age, what is the maximum age allowed? _____

36. Do you have a delayed vocation program?

   _____(1 yes   _____(2 no

37. If you answer yes, indicate the following:

   _____ (1 year program began
   _____ (2 number of candidates at present
   _____ (3 are you satisfied with your program?

38. Comments: _____

   _____

39. Who is consulted about the candidate concerning her admission?

	Always	Sometimes	Never
1) Formation personnel	_____ (1	_____ (2	_____ (3
2) Provincial council	_____ (1	_____ (2	_____ (3
3) Professional psychiatrist	_____ (1	_____ (2	_____ (3
4) Professional psychologist	_____ (1	_____ (2	_____ (3
5) Medical doctor	_____ (1	_____ (2	_____ (3
6) Priest counsellor	_____ (1	_____ (2	_____ (3
7) Sister counsellor	_____ (1	_____ (2	_____ (3
8) Vocation director	_____ (1	_____ (2	_____ (3

9) Major superior (other than _____ (1 _____ (2 _____ (3
   one accepting candidate)
10) Other: (specify)

_____ _____ (1 _____ (2 _____ (3
_____ _____ _____ _____
_____ _____ _____ _____

40. In the process of screening for the year 1965, how many candidates fall under the following categories?
    ___ (1 Number of applicants   ___ (3 Number advised not to come
    ___ (2 Number of acceptances   ___ (4 Number who actually came

41. Of those admitted in 1955 and in 1965 how many had the following backgrounds:

    1955   1965
    _____ (1   _____ (1   No high school diploma
    _____ (2   _____ (2   High school diploma only
    _____ (3   _____ (3   Bachelor's degree
    _____ (4   _____ (4   Master's degree
    _____ (5   _____ (5   Doctoral degree
    _____ (6   _____ (6   Nursing degree
    _____ (7   _____ (7   Social work degree
    _____ (8   _____ (8   Professional degree other than nursing and and social work (e.g. law, etc.)
    _____ (9   _____ (9   Some college work (no degree)
    _____ (10 _____ (10 Other special training of a post high school nature (but no degree)

42. Have you any special educational or experience requirement for entrance? Check as many categories as apply.
    _____(1 high school diploma
    _____(2 B.A., or equivalent
    _____(3 other educational requirement
    _____(4 some college work
    _____(5 some employment experience
    _____(6 other: (specify) _____

43. If other educational requirement is checked, i.e., No. 3 above, please specify:

    _____
    _____

VI. TRAINING PROGRAM

44. How long is your current formation program, 1965-1966?

	Years	Months
1) aspirancy or candidacy	_____ (1	_____ (1
2) postulancy	_____ (2	_____ (2
3) novitiate	_____ (3	_____ (3
4) juniorate or scholasticate (include only the period of formal educational training prior to going out on assignment)	_____ (4	_____ (4
5) time after juniorate program to profession of perpetual vows	_____ (5	_____ (5

45. Have you made any substantial changes in the length of the training program in the past ten years? Please check below.

	Eliminated	Shortened	Extended	Revised
1) aspirancy or candidacy	_____ (1	_____ (1	_____ (1	_____ (1
2) postulancy	_____ (2	_____ (2	_____ (2	_____ (2
3) novitiate	_____ (3	_____ (3	_____ (3	_____ (3
4) juniorate or scholasticate	_____ (4	_____ (4	_____ (4	_____ (4

46. Please describe briefly the changes made: _____
_____

47. Is a special noncollege program offered for those without college ability? _____(1 yes _____(2 no

48. If yes, please describe briefly _____
_____

49. In what areas of study are sisters under your jurisdiction currently studying for masters' and doctoral degrees?

Area of study	Institution	Number of sisters	
		Master's	Doctor's
_____ (1	_____ (1	_____ (1	_____ (1
_____ (2	_____ (2	_____ (2	_____ (2
_____ (3	_____ (3	_____ (3	_____ (3
_____ (4	_____ (4	_____ (4	_____ (4
_____ (5	_____ (5	_____ (5	_____ (5
_____ (6	_____ (6	_____ (6	_____ (6

	(7		(7		(7		(7
	(8		(8		(8		(8
	(9		(9		(9		(9
	(10		(10		(10		(10
	(11		(11		(11		(11
	(12		(12		(12		(12
	(13		(13		(13		(13
	(14		(14		(14		(14
	(15		(15		(15		(15

50. From what institutions have your sisters already received masters' and doctoral degrees between 1955 and 1965?

Institution	1955 - 1960 No. of sisters		1961 - 1965 No. of sisters	
	Master's	Doctor's	Master's	Doctor's
_____(1	____ (1	____ (1	____ (1	____ (1
_____(2	____ (2	____ (2	____ (2	____ (2
_____(3	____ (3	____ (3	____ (3	____ (3
_____(4	____ (4	____ (4	____ (4	____ (4
_____(5	____ (5	____ (5	____ (5	____ (5
_____(6	____ (6	____ (6	____ (6	____ (6
_____(7	____ (7	____ (7	____ (7	____ (7
_____(8	____ (8	____ (8	____ (8	____ (8
_____(9	____ (9	____ (9	____ (9	____ (9
_____(10	____ (10	____ (10	____ (10	____ (10
_____(11	____ (11	____ (11	____ (11	____ (11
_____(12	____ (12	____ (12	____ (12	____ (12
_____(13	____ (13	____ (13	____ (13	____ (13
_____(14	____ (14	____ (14	____ (14	____ (14
_____(15	____ (15	____ (15	____ (15	____ (15
_____(16	____ (16	____ (16	____ (16	____ (16
_____(17	____ (17	____ (17	____ (17	____ (17
_____(18	____ (18	____ (18	____ (18	____ (18
_____(19	____ (19	____ (19	____ (19	____ (19
_____(20	____ (20	____ (20	____ (20	____ (20

51. How many sisters are currently released for full-time study on the graduate level?

_____(1 Studying but not for degree

_____(3 Studying for doctor's degree

_____(2 Studying for a master's degree

_____(4 Studying for other professional degree

52. How many sisters are currently doing part-time study on the graduate level?

_____ (1 Studying but not for degree _____ (3 Studying for doctor's degree

_____ (2 Studying for a master's degree _____ (4 Studying for other professional degree

53. Do you have any sisters who are in training programs for administrative work? _____ (1 yes _____ (2 no

54. If yes, please indicate how many sisters are in these programs and for how long they are in training?

No. of sisters	Type of Program	Length of Training Programs		
		a few weeks or less	months	a year or more
_____	(1 Superiors	_____ (1	_____ (1	_____ (1
_____	(2 Elementary school principals	_____ (2	_____ (2	_____ (2
_____	(3 Secondary school principals	_____ (3	_____ (3	_____ (3
_____	(4 Special schools	_____ (4	_____ (4	_____ (4
_____	(5 College presidents	_____ (5	_____ (5	_____ (5
_____	(6 College deans	_____ (6	_____ (6	_____ (6
_____	(7 Hospital administration	_____ (7	_____ (7	_____ (7
_____	(8 Supervisors	_____ (8	_____ (8	_____ (8
_____	(9 other _____	_____ (9	_____ (9	_____ (9

(We expect this number to overlap with preceding questions.)

VII. SEPARATION

55. How many sisters left your congregation in the years specified? Please indicate the number for that year only. Include each sister only once.

	Before perpetual vows		After perpetual vows	
	Non-renewal of vows	Exclaus-tration	Seculari-zation	Exclaus-tration
1) 1950	_____ (1	_____ (1	_____ (1	_____ (1
2) 1955	_____ (2	_____ (2	_____ (2	_____ (2
3) 1960	_____ (3	_____ (3	_____ (3	_____ (3

4) 1963	_____ (4	_____ (4	_____ (4	_____ (4
5) 1965	_____ (5	_____ (5	_____ (5	_____ (5

56. What do you consider the main reasons why sisters who have not yet made perpetual vows leave your congregation? Please check.

Reason for leaving	very frequent	frequent	seldom	never
1) no vocation	_____(1	_____(2	_____(3	_____(4
2) weak formation	_____(1	_____(2	_____(3	_____(4
3) preference for marriage	_____(1	_____(2	_____(3	_____(4
4) dissatisfaction with community life	_____(1	_____(2	_____(3	_____(4
5) interest in different mode of apostolate	_____(1	_____(2	_____(3	_____(4
6) failure to achieve personal fulfillment	_____(1	_____(2	_____(3	_____(4
7) psychological disturbance	_____(1	_____(2	_____(3	_____(4
8) completion of professional training	_____(1	_____(2	_____(3	_____(4
9) no clear reasons	_____(1	_____(2	_____(3	_____(4
10) other: (specify) _____	_____(1	_____(2	_____(3	_____(4

57. What do you consider the main reasons why sisters who have made perpetual vows leave your congregation? Please check.

Reason for leaving	very frequent	frequent	seldom	never
1) no vocation	_____(1	_____(2	_____(3	_____(4
2) weak formation	_____(1	_____(2	_____(3	_____(4
3) preference for marriage	_____(1	_____(2	_____(3	_____(4
4) dissatisfaction with community life	_____(1	_____(2	_____(3	_____(4
5) interest in different mode of apostolate	_____(1	_____(2	_____(3	_____(4
6) failure to achieve personal fulfillment	_____(1	_____(2	_____(3	_____(4
7) psychological disturbance	_____(1	_____(2	_____(3	_____(4
8) completion of professional training	_____(1	_____(2	_____(3	_____(4

9) no clear reasons   ____(1 ____(2 ____(3 ____(4

10) other: (specify)

_____ ____(1 ____(2 ____(3 ____(4

58. Of the sisters who have left your congregation in the past five years, what percentage was recommended by the congregation to leave? (Answer for your province or the entire congregation if there are no provinces) _____

59. What is the procedure in your congregation when a sister leaves the congregation? Please check.

Procedure	In practice 10 years ago	In practice now
1) Sister leaves from motherhouse or from some community away from local house in secrecy	_____ (1	_____ (1
2) Sister leaves from motherhouse or from some community away from local house with the knowledge of her sisters	_____ (2	_____ (2
3) Sister leaves from local house in secrecy	_____ (3	_____ (3
4) Sister leaves from local house with the knowledge of her sisters but not in their presence.	_____ (4	_____ (4
5) Sister leaves from local house with the sisters present to say good-bye	_____ (5	_____ (5
6) other: (specify) _____	_____ (6	_____ (6

60. How are the members of your congregation informed about the departure of a sister from the congregation? Please check.

_____(1 Rumor

_____(2 Community newsletter

_____(3 Formal announcement to the local community in which the sister lived.

_____(4 Formal letter to each house

_____(5 Other: (specify)

_____

_____

61. Are there any restrictions on contacts between the sisters and former members of the congregation?

	In practice ten years ago	In practice now
1) forbidden	_____(1	_____(1
2) discouraged	_____(2	_____(2
3) tolerated	_____(3	_____(3
4) encouraged	_____(4	_____(4
5) other: (specify)		
_____ _____	_____(5	_____(5
_____ _____		

62. When a sister asks to leave the congregation what procedures are followed? Please indicate which ones you have found to be helpful.

	Always	Sometimes	Never	:	Very helpful	Somewhat helpful	Least helpful
1) Sister is sent on a vacation	__ (1	__ (2	__ (3	:	__ (1	__ (2	__ (3
2) Sister is given a change of assignment	__ (1	__ (2	__ (3	:	__ (1	__ (2	__ (3
3) Sister is offered professional counselling	__ (1	__ (2	__ (3	:	__ (1	__ (2	__ (3
4) Consideration is is given to those factors in the congregation's way of life which have disturbed the sister	__ (1	__ (2	__ (3	:	__ (1	__ (2	__ (3
5) If a sister has often expressed strong dissatisfaction with community life, she is encouraged to leave	__ (1	__ (2	__ (3	:	__ (1	__ (2	__ (3
6) Other: (specify)							
_____	__ (1	__ (2	__ (3	:	__ (1	__ (2	__ (3
_____	__	__	__	:	__	__	__

VIII. GOVERNMENT

63. In which of the following ways are local superiors assigned to office?

	always	sometimes	never
1) elected by the community she will serve	＿＿ (1	＿＿ (2	＿＿ (3
2) elected by all the members of the province.	＿＿ (1	＿＿ (2	＿＿ (3
3) appointed by the major superior from nominees submitted by all the members of the province.	＿＿ (1	＿＿ (2	＿＿ (3
4) appointed by the major superior in consultation with members of the province	＿＿ (1	＿＿ (2	＿＿ (3
5) appointed by the major superior in consultation with her council	＿＿ (1	＿＿ (2	＿＿ (3
6) appointed by the major superior without any specific consultation	＿＿ (1	＿＿ (2	＿＿ (3
7) other: (specify) ＿＿＿＿＿＿＿＿＿＿ ＿＿＿＿＿＿＿＿＿＿	＿＿ (1	＿＿ (2	＿＿ (3

64. Have you any special training for newly appointed superiors?

	In practice ten years ago	In practice now
1) Always	＿＿＿＿(1	＿＿＿＿(1
2) Usually	＿＿＿＿(2	＿＿＿＿(2
3) Occasionally	＿＿＿＿(3	＿＿＿＿(3
4) Never	＿＿＿＿(4	＿＿＿＿(4

65. After the expiration of a given term of office, does the superior return to ordinary community life as a subject?

	In practice ten years ago	In practice now
1) Always	＿＿＿＿(1	＿＿＿＿(1
2) Usually	＿＿＿＿(2	＿＿＿＿(2
3) Occasionally	＿＿＿＿(3	＿＿＿＿(3
4) Never	＿＿＿＿(4	＿＿＿＿(4

66. Are superiors ordinarily regarded de facto as principals or administrators?

	In practice ten years ago	In practice now
1) Always	_____(1	_____(1
2) Usually	_____(2	_____(2
3) Occasionally	_____(3	_____(3
4) Never	_____(4	_____(4

67. How are the local councillors selected for office?

	always	sometimes	never
1) chosen by local sisters	____ (1	____ (2	____ (3
2) chosen by Provincial Superior on the recommendations of local sisters	____ (1	____ (2	____ (3
3) chosen by Provincial Superior without recommendations	____ (1	____ (2	____ (3
4) appointed by the Superior General in consultation with Provincial Superior	____ (1	____ (2	____ (3
5) appointed by the Superior General without any specific consultation	____ (1	____ (2	____ (3
6) other: (specify) _____	____ (1	____ (2	____ (3

68. How do sisters represent their views in policy formation within the province now? Please check.

	Most usual	Accepted and quite usual	Accepted but unusual	Most unusual	Never
1) by direct letter from sister to Provincial Superior	___ (1	___ (2	___ (3	___ (4	___ (5
2) by letter from several sisters to Provincial Superior	___ (1	___ (2	___ (3	___ (4	___ (5
3) through a committee appointed just for this purpose.	___ (1	___ (2	___ (3	___ (4	___ (5
4) through a standing committee whose purpose it is to handle policy suggestions.	___ (1	___ (2	___ (3	___ (4	___ (5

5) no planned
method   ___ (1 ___ (2 ___ (3 ___ (4 ___ (5

6) other: (specify)

_____   ___ (1 ___ (2 ___ (3 ___ (4 ___ (5

_____   ___ ___ ___ ___ ___

69. How did sisters represent their views in policy formation within the province ten years ago? Please check.

	Most usual	Accepted and quite usual	Accepted but unusual	Most unusual	Never
1) by direct letter from sister to Provincial Superior	___ (1	___ (2	___ (3	___ (4	___ (5
2) by letter from several sisters to Provincial Superior	___ (1	___ (2	___ (3	___ (4	___ (5
3) through a committee appointed just for this purpose.	___ (1	___ (2	___ (3	___ (4	___ (5
4) through a standing committee whose purpose it is to handle policy suggestions.	___ (1	___ (2	___ (3	___ (4	___ (5
5) no planned method	___ (1	___ (2	___ (3	___ (4	___ (5
6) other: (specify) _____	___ (1	___ (2	___ (3	___ (4	___ (5
_____	___	___	___	___	___

70. Do you have an advisory board?

	Elected Yes	No	Appointed Yes	No
1) for local affairs	___ (1	___ (2	___ (1	___ (2
2) for provincial affairs	___ (1	___ (2	___ (1	___ (2
3) for total congregational affairs	___ (1	___ (2	___ (1	___ (2

71. Which of the following procedures is used for chapter preparation in your congregation?

	ten years ago			:	now		
	always	sometimes	never	:	always	sometimes	never
1) Provincial Chapter of Affairs is preceded by a Local Chapter of Affairs in each house.	___ (1	___ (2	___ (3	:	___ (1	___ (2	___ (3
2) There is a Provincial Chapter of Affairs and elections, but no Local Chapter of Affairs.	___ (1	___ (2	___ (3	:	___ (1	___ (2	___ (3
3) There is no Provincial Chapter of Affairs, but there is a Provincial Chapter for the election of delegates to the General Chapter.	___ (1	___ (2	___ (3	:	___ (1	___ (2	___(3

(Chapter of Affairs here means a meeting wherein attention is given to the review of policy and the making of new policy.)

72. In which of the following ways are Provincial Superiors assigned to office?

	always	sometimes	never
1) elected by all the members of the province	_____ (1	_____ (2	_____ (3
2) elected by members of Provincial Chapter	_____ (1	_____ (2	_____ (3
3) appointed by the major superior from nominees submitted by all the members of the province	_____ (1	_____ (2	_____ (3
4) appointed by the major superior in consultation with members of the province.	_____ (1	_____ (2	_____ (3

5) appointed by major superior in
consultation with her council   _____ (1 _____ (2 _____ (3

6) appointed by major superior with-
out any specific consultation   _____ (1 _____ (2 _____ (3

7) other: (specify)

_____   ____ (1 _____ (2 _____ (3

_____   ____   ____   ____

73. Which of the following kinds of information are solicited and
considered by the Provincial Chapter of Affairs?

	solicited			:	considered		
	always	sometimes	never	:	always	sometimes	never
1) suggestions from individual houses and from individual sisters.	___ (1	___ (2	___ (3	:	___ (1	___ (2	___ (3
2) suggestions from individual sisters only	___ (1	___ (2	___ (3	:	___ (1	___ (2	___ (3
3) suggestions from individual houses only	___ (1	___ (2	___ (3	:	___ (1	___ (2	___ (3
4) suggestions from elected representatives only	___ (1	___ (2	___ (3	:	___ (1	___ (2	___ (3
5) other: (specify) _____	___ (1	___ (2	___ (3	:	___ (1	___ (2	___ (3

74. Who constitutes the membership of the Provincial Chapter?

	No. by election	No. by appointment	No. ex officio
1) total number of sisters	_____ (1	_____ (1	_____ (1
2) number of superiors only	_____ (2	_____ (2	_____ (2
3) number of sisters with perpetual vows	_____ (3	_____ (3	_____ (3
4) number of sisters with temporary vows	_____ (4	_____ (4	_____ (4
5) other: (specify) _____	_____ (5	_____ (5	_____ (5

75. When was your last Provincial Chapter held?   _____(1

76. When will your next Provincial Chapter be held?   _____(2

77. Will this be a regular or special chapter?

    _____(1 regular   _____(2 special

78. How do local sisters participate in the election of the Superior General?

    _____(1 indirectly through the election of representatives for the Provincial Chapter only
    _____(2 indirectly through the election of representatives for the General Chapter
    _____(3 direct vote but with no pre-discussion of candidates
    _____(4 planned consideration of candidates prior to direct vote
    _____(5 other: (specify) _____

79. At present, how do the local sisters present their ideas for a General Chapter?

    1) A formal structure exists for communication between sisters and representatives   _____(1
    2) No formal structure but communication among sisters and representatives is encouraged   _____(2
    3) Sisters are asked to submit proposals to the chapter committees   _____(3
    4) Sisters are asked to fill out questionnaires which survey their views   _____(4
    5) other: (specify)

    _____   _____(5

80. How do your present procedures for presenting ideas of the sisters for the General Chapter compare with procedures for your last General Chapter?

    identical ____(1   somewhat changed ____(2   notably changed ____(3

81. Which of the following kinds of information are solicited and considered by the General Chapter of Affairs?

	solicited			:	considered		
	always	sometimes	never	:	always	sometimes	never
1) suggestions from individual houses and from individual sisters	___ (1	___ (2	___ (3	:	___ (1	___ (2	___ (3

2) suggestions from
individual sisters
only — (1 — (2 — (3 : — (1 — (2 — (3

3) suggestions from
individual houses
only — (1 — (2 — (3 : — (1 — (2 — (3

4) suggestions from
provinces only — (1 — (2 — (3 : — (1 — (2 — (3

5) suggestions from
elected represen-
tatives only — (1 — (2 — (3 : — (1 — (2 — (3

6) other: (specify)
_____ — (1 — (2 — (3 : — (1 — (2 — (3

82. Is it obligatory in your congregation for the General Chapter to consider all suggestions from:

	yes	no
1) Provincial Chapters	_____ (1	_____ (2
2) local chapters	_____ (1	_____ (2
3) individual sisters	_____ (1	_____ (2

83. Is a general report of all suggestions made to the sisters after the General Chapter?   _____(1 yes   _____(2 no

84. If yes, what form does the report take?

	complete report	selected report
1) a circular to each sister	_____(1	_____(2
2) a circular to each house	_____(1	_____(2
3) a circular to each province, and and then to the houses at the will of the provincial	_____(1	_____(2
4) other: (specify) _____	_____(1	_____(2

85. When was your last General Chapter held?   _____(1

86. When will your next General Chapter be held?   _____(2

87. Will this be a regular or special chapter?
_____(1 regular   _____(2 special

88. How are you preparing for your next chapter? Please indicate what plans you have made by checking the following items.

Preparation for chapter	Now doing or have done	Plan to do	Not doing
1) scheduled discussions in local communities	_____ (1	_____ (2	_____ (3
2) formation of committees to work on various areas of structures in the religious life, e.g., vows, formation, common life, government	_____ (1	_____ (2	_____ (3
3) surveys	_____ (1	_____ (2	_____ (3
4) soliciting suggestions in a general letter to the whole congregation	_____ (1	_____ (2	_____ (3
5) spiritual preparation in the form of intensive theological and scriptural courses and lectures	_____ (1	_____ (2	_____ (3
6) studies of canon law	_____ (1	_____ (2	_____ (3
7) encouragement of inter-house dialogue in preparation for chapter	_____ (1	_____ (2	_____ (3
8) encouragement of intra-house dialogue in preparation for chapter	_____ (1	_____ (2	_____ (3

89. How does your current General Chapter preparation differ from the preparation of earlier chapters?

_____(1 a great deal   _____(2 somewhat   _____(3 not at all

90. How many representatives does each province have for the General Chapter?

_____(1   _____(2   _____(3
by appointment   ex officio members   by election

91. Of the total membership of the General Chapter, what is the number of ex officio members and elected delegates?

_____(1   _____(2   _____(3
total members   ex officio   elected

92. Will the representation at the next General Chapter be similar to past chapters?   _____(1 yes   _____(2 no

93. If no, please check the ways in which the representation at your next General Chapter will be different:

_____(1 general membership enlarged
_____(2 number of elected delegates increased

_____(3 method for electing delegates changed
_____(4 other: (specify) _____

94. How many professed · sisters are there in your entire congregation? _____
(Include all sisters who have made vows, even those who have only made their first vows.)

95. What is the total number of sisters in your province? ____

IX. CHANGE

96. What changes has your congregation introduced into the liturgy?

	All convents			Some convents			No
	always	some-times	never :	always	some-times	never :	con-vents
1) altar facing people	__(1	__(2	__(3 :	__(1	__(2	__(3 :	__(4
2) English hymns sung at daily Mass	__(1	__(2	__(3 :	__(1	__(2	__(3 :	__(4
3) bidding prayers	__(1	__(2	__(3 :	__(1	__(2	__(3 :	__(4
4) spontaneous bidding prayers	__(1	__(2	__(3 :	__(1	__(2	__(3 :	__(4
5) homily	__(1	__(2	__(3 :	__(1	__(2	__(3 :	__(4
6) congregational meal after Mass	__(1	__(2	__(3 :	__(1	__(2	__(3 :	__(4
7) offertory procession	__(1	__(2	__(3 :	__(1	__(2	__(3 :	__(4
8) instruments (other than organ)	__(1	__(2	__(3 :	__(1	__(2	__(3 :	__(4
9) kiss of peace	__(1	__(2	__(3 :	__(1	__(2	__(3 :	__(4
10) other: (specify)							
_____	__(1	__(2	__(3 :	__(1	__(2	__(3 :	__(4
_____	__	__	__ :	__	__	__ :	__

97. By whom are arrangements for the annual retreat usually made?

	ten years ago		:	now		
	always	sometimes	never :	always	sometimes	never
1) Provincial Superior	__ (1	__ (2	__ (3 :	__ (1	__ (2	__ (3
2) local superior	__ (1	__ (2	__ (3 :	__ (1	__ (2	__ (3
3) local community decision	__ (1	__ (2	__ (3 :	__ (1	__ (2	__ (3

4) individual choice ___ (1 ___ (2 ___ (3 : ___ (1 ___ (2 ___ (3
5) other: (specify)
_____ ___ (1 ___ (2 ___ (3 : ___ (1 ___ (2 ___ (3

98. What qualities do you look for in persons you choose to direct your formation program?

	always	sometimes	never
1) knowledge of theology	___ (1	___ (2	___ (3
2) understanding of human psychology	___ (1	___ (2	___ (3
3) deeply rooted in the tradition of the congregation	___ (1	___ (2	___ (3
4) orientated toward innovation in the liturgy	___ (1	___ (2	___ (3
5) orientated to innovation in styles of community	___ (1	___ (2	___ (3
6) concerned with the preservation of the congregation's customs and ideas	___ (1	___ (2	___ (3
7) regularity of life	___ (1	___ (2	___ (3
8) orderliness of personal effects	___ (1	___ (2	___ (3
9) a splendid generosity	___ (1	___ (2	___ (3
10) other: (specify)			
_____	___ (1	___ (2	___ (3

99. Do you seek the same qualities in your formation personnel now that were looked for ten years ago in your congregation's formation personnel?

_____(1 yes   _____(2 no

100. If no, what is the difference? _____
_____

101. How are your formation personnel selected?

	always	sometimes	never
1) appointed by the Superior General with recommendation of Provincial Superior	___ (1	___ (2	___ (3
2) appointed by Superior General with recommendation by council or province	___ (1	___ (2	___ (3

3) appointed by Superior General
after informal discussions with
persons of her own selection _____ (1 _____ (2 _____ (3
4) other: (specify)

_____ _____ (1 _____ (2 _____ (3

102. Do your sisters keep their own names as their religious names?
(Own name refers to baptismal and surname.)

_____1) have always used their own names
_____2) plan to change to use of own names
_____3) have already changed to use of own names
_____4) new sisters will use own names
_____5) have not considered the use of own names

103. Please specify any government or local civic programs that
your congregation has participated in during 1965 or 1966?

	1965	1966	:		1965	1966
1) Headstart	__(1	__(1	: 7) Special educ.		__(7	__(7
2) Neighborhood			: 8) Subsidized			
Youth Corps	__(2	__(2	: welfare prog.		__(8	__(8
3) Upward Bound	__(3	__(3	: 9) Subsidized			
4) Subsidized			: hospital prog.		__(9	__(9
summer center			: 10) Subsidized			
in city	__(4	__(4	: teaching ma-			
5) Subsidized			: terials pro-			
summer center			: gram includ-			
in suburb	__(5	__(5	: ing libraries		__(10	__(10
6) Subsidized			: 11) Subsidized			
summer center			: lunch			
in rural center	__(6	__(6	: program		__(11	__(11
			: 12) other: (specify)			
			: _____		__(12	__(12

104. Has there been a major revision of your Rule or Constitution in
the last five years?

_____(1 yes   _____(2 no

105. If yes, what year?   _____

106. Are you planning another revision of your Rule or
Constitution?

_____(1 yes   _____(2 no

107. If yes, approximately when _____

108. What major changes do you have in mind?
     Proposed constitutional changes:

     _____
     _____
     _____

109. What kinds of on-going evaluation of personnel in their work-situations does your congregation have?

	always	occasionally
1) Use of professionally-trained supervisors	_____ (1	_____ (2
2) Use of supervisors, but not professionally trained	_____ (1	_____ (2
3) Recommendations for a sister's change of work based on the sister's request	_____ (1	_____ (2
4) Change of sisters to new work or retirement based on recommendation of superiors	_____ (1	_____ (2
5) Change of sisters to new work or retirement based on recommendation of supervisors	_____ (1	_____ (2
6) Systematic assessment of work performance prior to recommendation for change of work	_____ (1	_____ (2
7) other: (specify)	_____ (1	_____ (2
_____	_____	_____

110. Are you reassessing your methods of transfer of sisters?
     _____(1 yes   _____(2 no

111. If yes, will you describe the direction in which you plan to move or have already moved:
     Plans for new methods of transfer:

     _____
     _____

112. Have there been any changes in your religious habit in the past five years?
     _____(1 none   _____(2 minor   _____(3 major

113. Are you planning changes in your religious habit in the next five years?

_____(1 none   _____(2 minor   _____(3 major

114. If there have been changes in your religious habit in the last five years, by whom were the decisions made to effect the change?

	decision to change	choice of style
1) by the major superior alone	_____ (1	_____ (1
2) by the major superior in consultation with her council	_____ (2	_____ (2
3) at a chapter but with no previous consultation with the sisters	_____ (3	_____ (3
4) at a chapter with a previous polling of all the sisters	_____ (4	_____ (4
5) by the direct vote of the entire congregation	_____ (5	_____ (5
6) other: (specify) _____	_____ (6	_____ (6

115. In which of the following areas have changes been made? What experiments have been undertaken or abandoned within the last two years: Please check.

	changes made	experiments begun	experiments halted
1) horarium	_____ (1	_____ (2	_____ (3
2) silence	_____ (1	_____ (2	_____ (3
3) recreation	_____ (1	_____ (2	_____ (3
4) chapter of faults	_____ (1	_____ (2	_____ (3
5) regulations for participation in extra-community activities	_____ (1	_____ (2	_____ (3
6) participation of laity and religious who are not members of the local house in community Mass	_____ (1	_____ (2	_____ (3
7) participation of people who are not members of the local house in community meals	_____ (1	_____ (2	_____ (3
8) participation of people who are not members of the local house in community recreations	_____ (1	_____ (2	_____ (3
9) encouraging friendships	_____ (1	_____ (2	_____ (3
10) experimenting with personal budgets	_____ (1	_____ (2	_____ (3

11) community decision making _____ (1 _____ (2 _____ (3
12) other _____ _____ (1 _____ (2 _____ (3
13) other _____ _____ (1 _____ (2 _____ (3

116. Looking forward to the next ten years, which of the following developments do you expect to see?

	no	yes	uncertain
1) an increase in the number of vocations	_____ (1	_____ (2	_____ (3
2) continued expansion of foundations	_____ (1	_____ (2	_____ (3
3) continuation of essentially the same works	_____ (1	_____ (2	_____ (3
4) more involvement in civic and national programs	_____ (1	_____ (2	_____ (3
5) more involvement in public protests	_____ (1	_____ (2	_____ (3
6) greater voice for sisters in planning	_____ (1	_____ (2	_____ (3
7) basic changes in types of work in education	_____ (1	_____ (2	_____ (3
8) basic changes in types of work in health	_____ (1	_____ (2	_____ (3
9) basic changes in types of work in welfare	_____ (1	_____ (2	_____ (3
10) basic changes in style of religious life	_____ (1	_____ (2	_____ (3
11) none of these	_____ (1	_____ (2	_____ (3
12) other: (specify)			

117. Which of the following kinds of reading is customarily encouraged among sisters by their religious superiors?
_____ (1 news magazines   _____ (5 diocesan paper
_____ (2 news commentaries   _____ (6 spiritual reading books
_____ (3 religious journals   _____ (7 professional journals
_____ (4 daily newspaper   _____ (8 other: (specify)
_____

118. Which of the following news media would you recommend to your sisters to read?

	very highly	highly	moderately	not at all
1) Sunday New York Times Magazine	____ (1	____ (2	____ (3	____ (4

2) Time	___ (1	___ (2	___ (3	___ (4
3) Newsweek	___ (1	___ (2	___ (3	___ (4
4) U.S. News and World Report	___ (1	___ (2	___ (3	___ (4
5) New Republic	___ (1	___ (2	___ (3	___ (4
6) National Review	___ (1	___ (2	___ (3	___ (4
7) National Catholic Reporter	___ (1	___ (2	___ (3	___ (4
8) Commonweal	___ (1	___ (2	___ (3	___ (4
9) America	___ (1	___ (2	___ (3	___ (4
10) Ave Maria	___ (1	___ (2	___ (3	___ (4
11) U.S. Catholic	___ (1	___ (2	___ (3	___ (4
12) Jubilee	___ (1	___ (2	___ (3	___ (4
13) Diocesan Paper	___ (1	___ (2	___ (3	___ (4
14) None of these	___ (1	___ (2	___ (3	___ (4
15) other: (specify)				
_____	___ (1	___ (2	___ (3	___ (4

119. What new works have you added to your apostolic activities in the past two years which you consider oriented to the expectations expressed in the "Pastoral Constitution on the Church in the Modern World?"

New Works:

1) _____
2) _____
3) _____
4) _____
5) _____

120. Check the following conditions which you regard as barriers to the effective development of new roles for your sisters.

_____(1 lack of preparation   _____(4 lack of awareness of
_____(2 pressure of time due to   contemporary situation
      current works   _____(5 other: (specify)
_____(3 community works
                                          _____

121. Check the following conditions which you regard as barriers to the effective development of the present roles filled by your sisters.

_____(1 lack of preparation   _____(4 lack of awareness of
_____(2 pressure of time due to   contemporary situation
      current works   _____(5 other: (specify)
_____(3 community works

122. Which of the following sources do you perceive will be the major determinants of changes you will make in the next five years? Put a (4) beside that which you consider very influential in regard to change; put a (3) beside that which is less influential; put a (2) beside that which is somewhat influential; put a (1) beside that which is of minor influence.

    _____(1 the ideas of the sisters
    _____(2 the directives of the Sacred Congregation of Religious
    _____(3 the original intentions of the founder of the congregation
    _____(4 the decrees of Vatican II
    _____(5 other: (specify)

    _____

123. Which of the following do you perceive are the most pressing needs of this moment? Put 4, 3, 2, 1 as in directions in question 122 above.

    _____(1   cooperation with the directives from the Sacred Congregation
    _____(2   circumspection in superiors and patience in subjects
    _____(3   intensification of efforts to achieve personal sanctity
    _____(4   careful study of society
    _____(5   careful study of theological developments
    _____(6   constant effort to open channels of communication
    _____(7   greater appreciation on the part of the young religious for the achievements of the past
    _____(8   intense examination of the relevancy of the gospel to the current conditions of the world
    _____(9   deeper knowledge of the spirit of the founder
    _____(10 development of a basically new liturgical life
    _____(11 experiments with new kinds of community life

124. Are you experimenting with any new ways of living community life?

    _____(1 yes   _____(2 no

125. If yes, please describe: _____

    _____
    _____
    _____

126. Are you experimenting with any new works?

_____(1 yes _____(2 no

127. If yes, please describe and indicate how many of your sisters the changes will effect?

Changes: _____

_____

_____

_____

_____

_____

_____

128. If your congregation has divided into provinces within the last twenty years. please indicate the year in which this occurred.

_____ year

129. Have you yet received the directives of the Post-Conciliar Commission on Religious Life: _____(1 yes _____(2 no

130. At what institutions are sisters under your jurisdiction currently studying for master's and doctoral degrees?

Institution:	Number of sisters	
	Master's	Doctor's
_____(1	_____ (1	_____ (1
_____(2	_____ (2	_____ (2
_____(3	_____ (3	_____ (3
_____(4	_____ (4	_____ (4
_____(5	_____ (5	_____ (5
_____(6	_____ (6	_____ (6
_____(7	_____ (7	_____ (7
_____(8	_____ (8	_____ (8
_____(9	_____ (9	_____ (9
_____(10	_____ (10	_____ (10
_____(11	_____ (11	_____ (11
_____(12	_____ (12	_____ (12
_____(13	_____ (13	_____ (13
_____(14	_____ (14	_____ (14
_____(15	_____ (15	_____ (15

131. In what areas of study have your sisters already received masters' and doctoral degrees between 1956 and 1965?

Area of study:	1956 - 1960 Number of sisters		1961 - 1965 Number of sisters	
	Master's	Doctor's	Master's	Doctor's
_____(1	___ (1	___ (1	___ (1	___ (1
_____(2	___ (2	___ (2	___ (2	___ (2
_____(3	___ (3	___ (3	___ (3	___ (3
_____(4	___ (4	___ (4	___ (4	___ (4
_____(5	___ (5	___ (5	___ (5	___ (5
_____(6	___ (6	___ (6	___ (6	___ (6
_____(7	___ (7	___ (7	___ (7	___ (7
_____(8	___ (8	___ (8	___ (8	___ (8
_____(9	___ (9	___ (9	___ (9	___ (9
_____(10	___ (10	___ (10	___ (10	___ (10
_____(11	___ (11	___ (11	___ (11	___ (11
_____(12	___ (12	___ (12	___ (12	___ (12

132. Where and when was your religious order founded?
Country _____(1   Year _____(2

133. Where is your motherhouse presently located? _____

We are deeply grateful to you for your cooperation in this very important survey. We will do everything we can to get the results back to you in time for your present and future planning.

Sincerely yours,
THE RESEARCH COMMITTEE

* * * * * * * * * * * * * * * *

Please use the reverse side for comments. Be sure to mark the *number* of the *question* to which your comment applies.

Congregational Survey — 1982 LCWR

Emmanuel College
Sociology Department
400 The Fenway
Boston, MA 02115

Dear Sister Administrator:

It is now fifteen years since Part I of the Sisters' Survey came to each religious congregation in the summer of 1966. At that time 414 different congregations and/or provinces provided data to enable us to share in a comparative report on trends in membership, ministries, formation programs, education of sisters, property, health, government and future planning. In order to bring these data up to date and to provide each group (414 units) with a trend report, will you please have someone search your records to provide the needed information. There may be some items that do not apply to you and some for which you do not have as accurate information as you may wish to have. Estimates are better than no information, and filling in what you can find will be most helpful. Eight items call specifically for the opinion of the current administrative personnel. Will you kindly reserve these items for your own response. These are items 56, 57, 116, 118, 120, 122, 123, 135.

Your congregation number is _____.
This will appear on any documents that we send to you.
Please place this number on each page of this report. We
urge you to keep your number recorded in some safe
place for future reference. Your data are rendered anonymous in our files where they are identified only by this
number. All researchers who work with these data have
access only to that number.

Some questions will appear outdated because so many
changes have occurred since 1966. Please be patient with
us in these instances because we want to be able to report
as accurately as possible what changes have occurred.
There are some new items without corresponding 1966
forms.

Your cooperation is deeply appreciated. It will enable all
of us to have an accurate record of change and continuity.
Your responses will be compared with your own 1966
responses if your group participated at that time and with
the national totals. The results will be useful to you for
planning the future with an accurate foundation of useful
facts

The Research Team

1. Are you responding for an entire congregation or for a single province?

   1. Congregation without provinces _____
   2. Province _____
   3. Congregation with provinces _____
   4. Other (please specify) _____

2. How many provinces did your congregation have in 1966 and how many does it have now? (Kindly insert either the word "none" or the number of provinces).

   In 1966 _____ (USA only)   In 1981 _____ (USA only)
   In 1966 _____ (entire world)   In 1981 _____ (entire world)

3. What kind of order is yours?

   1. Diocesan _____   2. Pontifical _____   3. Other (please specify):
   _____

4. In what states of the United States and in what foreign countries do you have sisters?

   A. United States   No.   No.

1. _____ _____	16. _____ _____
2. _____ _____	17. _____ _____
3. _____ _____	18. _____ _____
4. _____ _____	19. _____ _____
5. _____ _____	20. _____ _____
6. _____ _____	21. _____ _____
7. _____ _____	22. _____ _____
8. _____ _____	23. _____ _____
9. _____ _____	24. _____ _____
10. _____ _____	25. _____ _____
11. _____ _____	26. _____ _____
12. _____ _____	27. _____ _____
13. _____ _____	28. _____ _____
14. _____ _____	29. _____ _____
15. _____ _____	30. _____ _____

   B. Foreign Countries   No.   No.

1. _____ _____	11. _____ _____
2. _____ _____	12. _____ _____
3. _____ _____	13. _____ _____
4. _____ _____	14. _____ _____
5. _____ _____	15. _____ _____
6. _____ _____	16. _____ _____
7. _____ _____	17. _____ _____

8. _____ _____   18. _____ _____
9. _____ _____   19. _____ _____
10. _____._____   20. _____ _____

*This questionnaire is going to groups with and without provinces. If you are a congregation without provinces mark No. 1. If your group has provinces and you are answering for only one province mark No. 2. If all your records are centralized and you are answering for all the units, whether provinces or regions or other, mark No. 3. If your group is a different type unit mark No. 4 and explain.

6. What was the population of your group (province or congregation) as of November 1981?
   1. _____ All Sisters who have made perpetual vows
   2. _____ Sisters in initial commitment (i.e. those with vows or promises but not final commitment)
   3. _____ Novices (i.e. in canonical year)
   4. _____ Affiliates or postulants (i.e. accepted for entrance but pre-novitiate)
   5. _____ Candidates (i.e. those not yet actually accepted)

7a. How many sisters live now in rental housing in comparison to 1966?*
   No. of sisters _____ (1981) No. of units _____ (1981)
   No. of sisters _____ (1966) No. of units _____ (1966)

7b. How many community owned or leased automobiles do you have?*
   1966: owned _____ leased _____
   1981: owned _____ leased _____

*Where exact information is not available, use these phrases (regarding housing and cars).

None	About half as many as we have now	A few more than now
Scarcely any	Twenty percent less than now	Many more than now
A few	About the same as now	

I. WORK CATEGORIES

8. Please indicate the number of your sisters engaged on a full-time basis or part-time basis in the types of work listed below. There are five major categories:

A. Teaching and Educational Administration
B. Missionary and Catechetical Work
C. Health Care and Administration
D. Social Service
E. Special Staff Functions and Services

Be sure to look through all the categories before you start filling them in. We realize that some types of work can go under several names. What we ask is that you choose the listing which most closely describes the work a given sister does and list her only once for *that* work. If she works *part-time* in several areas, the sister will be listed in several different categories, but only one time for each specific type of work. In the *part-time* listings, therefore, the numbers you give may exceed the total number of persons within your congregation. In the full-time listing, a sister will be listed only once.

Should a work you do not fit under any of these categories, add it at the end of the questionnaire with the requested information.

8a. Teaching and Educational Administration

Time				Time		
Full	Part	Teaching in:		Full	Part	Teaching in:
1. __	1. __	pre-school (daycare)		7. __	7. __	school of nursing
2. __	2. __	elementary		8. __	8. __	secular college or university
3. __	3. __	private, parochial, diocesan high school of your congregation.*		9. __	9. __	adult education
				10. __	10. __	special education (e.g. retarded)
4. __	4. __	multi-staffed and/or co-sponsored high school		11. __	11. __	poverty programs (e.g. Headstart)
5. __	5. __	your congregation college		12. __	12. __	migrant education
6. __	6. __	inter-cong. or non-cong. Catholic college		13. __	13. __	other (specify) _____ _____ _____

Time			Time		
Full	**Part**	**Administration:**	**Full**	**Part**	**Administration:**
1. ___	1. ___	school	6. ___	6. ___	other (specify)
2. ___	2. ___	college			(e.g. school
3. ___	3. ___	nursing school			superintendent)
4. ___	4. ___	special program			_____
5. ___	5. ___	supervisor			_____

*Mark here if the school is defined as of your congregation even if lay faculty and sisters of other congregations teach there.

8b. Missionary and Catechetical Work

Time			Time		
Full	**Part**		**Full**	**Part**	
1. ___	1. ___	foreign missions	8. ___	8. ___	CCD teacher training
2. ___	2. ___	home missions			
3. ___	3. ___	convert work	9. ___	9. ___	catechetical materials development
4. ___	4. ___	retreat work			
5. ___	5. ___	CCD instruction for children and similar programs	10. ___	10. ___	House of Prayer, Renewal Center
6. ___	6. ___	campus ministry	11. ___	11. ___	other (specify)
7. ___	7. ___	adult catechetical centers			_____
					_____
					_____

8c. Health Care and Administration

Time			Time		
Full	**Part**	**Direct care as:**	**Full**	**Part**	**Direct care as:**
1. ___	1. ___	physician	6. ___	6. ___	dentist
2. ___	2. ___	professional nurse	7. ___	7. ___	dietitian
3. ___	3. ___	L.P.N.	8. ___	8. ___	pharmacist
4. ___	4. ___	psychiatrist	9. ___	9. ___	lab. technician
5. ___	5. ___	clinical psychologist	10. ___	10. ___	other (specify):
					_____
					_____

Time			Time		
Full	**Part**	**Administration:**	**Full**	**Part**	**Administration:**
1. ___	1. ___	hospital	4. ___	4. ___	nursing home
2. ___	2. ___	infirmary	5. ___	5. ___	other (specify):
3. ___	3. ___	clinic			_____
					_____

8d. Social Service

Full	Part		Full	Part	
1. __	1. __	school counseling	11. __	11. __	homes for orphans
2. __	2. __	family counseling	12. __	12. __	residence for working girls
3. __	3. __	social case work e.g. juvenile court	13. __	13. __	resident or guest house
4. __	4. __	medical social work	14. __	14. __	homes for delinquents
5. __	5. __	community organizing	15. __	15. __	homes for the aged
6. __	6. __	inner city programs (other than teaching)	16. __	16. __	administration of above-mentioned houses
7. __	7. __	group work (e.g. neighborhood house director)	17. __	17. __	family shelters, homes for battered women
8. __	8. __	home visiting program	18. __	18. __	drug abuse centers
9. __	9. __	neighborhood or settlement houses	19. __	19. __	other (specify):
10. __	10. __	maternity-infant homes			

8e. Special Staff Programs and Services

Full	Part	Staff within cong.:	Full	Part	Staff within cong.:
1. __	1. __	general administration	7. __	7. __	communications
2. __	2. __	provincial administration	8. __	8. __	archivist
3. __	3. __	formation programs	9. __	9. __	program for retired sisters
4. __	4. __	special programs e.g. tertian	10. __	10. __	research
5. __	5. __	vocation work	11. __	11. __	other (specify):
6. __	6. __	public relations			

Full	Part	On staff of national organization:	Full	Part	On staff of national organization:
1. __	1. __	NCEA, other Church organization	3. __	3. __	CCD
			4. __	4. __	religious formation
			5. __	5. __	a publication

2. ___ 2. ___ LCWR, NAWR,   6. ___   6. ___ other (specify):
other relig. gov. org.   _____
national or state   _____

Time			Time		
Full	Part	Library Services:	Full	Part	Library Services:
1. ___	1. ___	school librarian	4. ___	4. ___	medical records
2. ___	2. ___	college librarian			librarian
3. ___	3. ___	medical librarian	5. ___	5. ___	other (specify):

_____
_____

Time			Time		
Full	Part	Clerical Services:	Full	Part	Clerical Services:
1. ___	1. ___	business office	3. ___	3. ___	other (specify):
2. ___	2. ___	secretarial work			

_____
_____

Time			Time		
Full	Part	Other Services:	Full	Part	Other Services:
1. ___	1. ___	kitchen service	6. ___	6. ___	printing, binding
2. ___	2. ___	maintenance	7. ___	7. ___	altar preparations
3. ___	3. ___	housekeeper	8. ___	8. ___	receptionist
4. ___	4. ___	care of rectories,	9. ___	9. ___	other (specify):
		seminaries, etc.			
5. ___	5. ___	seamstress			

_____
_____

(Do not include ordinary housework every sister may do regularly.)

II. INSTITUTIONS

9. Please give the number of different institutions in which your sisters work, and which fall into the following categories:

Institution:	congregation owned	diocesan owned	parish owned	other (specify)
1. pre-school	1. ___	1. ___	1. ___	1. ___
2. elementary	2. ___	2. ___	2. ___	2. ___
3. high school	3. ___	3. ___	3. ___	3. ___
4. junior college	4. ___	4. ___	4. ___	4. ___
5. college	5. ___	5. ___	5. ___	5. ___
6. graduate school	6. ___	6. ___	6. ___	6. ___
7. nursing school	7. ___	7. ___	7. ___	7. ___
8. special school	8. ___	8. ___	8. ___	8. ___
9. religion center	9. ___	9. ___	9. ___	9. ___

10. retreat center	10. ___	10. ___	10. ___	10. _____
11. hospital	11. ___	11. ___	11. ___	11. _____
12. clinic	12. ___	12. ___	12. ___	12. _____
13. nursing home	13. ___	13. ___	13. ___	13. _____
14. social welfare center	14. ___	14. ___	14. ___	14. _____
15. maternity/infant home	15. ___	15. ___	15. ___	15. _____
16. child care center	16. ___	16. ___	16. ___	16. _____
17. home for orphans	17. ___	17. ___	17. ___	17. _____
18. home for delinquents	18. ___	18. ___	18. ___	18. _____
19. working-girls home	19. ___	19. ___	19. ___	19. _____
20. home for aged	20. ___	20. ___	20. ___	20. _____
21. guest house	21. ___	21. ___	21. ___	21. _____
22. community center	22. ___	22. ___	22. ___	22. _____
23. house of prayer	23. ___	23. ___	23. ___	23. _____

Other (specify):

24. _____	24. ___	24. ___	24. ___	24. _____
25. _____	25. ___	25. ___	25. ___	25. _____
26. _____	26. ___	26. ___	26. ___	26. _____
27. _____	27. ___	27. ___	27. ___	27. _____
28. _____	28. ___	28. ___	28. ___	28. _____
29. _____	29. ___	29. ___	29. ___	29. _____
30. _____	30. ___	30. ___	30. ___	30. _____
31. _____	31. ___	31. ___	31. ___	31. _____
32. _____	32. ___	32. ___	32. ___	32. _____

10. Please indicate the number of buildings your congregation (or province) leases, rents, or owns.

Buildings:	Owned	Leased	Rented
1. mother house	_____	_____	_____
2. provincial house	_____	_____	_____
3. pre-novitiate buildings	_____	_____	_____
4. novitiate	_____	_____	_____
5. juniorate	_____	_____	_____
6. other houses of study	_____	_____	_____
7. infirmary	_____	_____	_____
8. home for retired sisters	_____	_____	_____
9. retreat house	_____	_____	_____
10. vacation house	_____	_____	_____
11. guest house	_____	_____	_____
12. residence	_____	_____	_____
Other (specify):			
13. _____	_____	_____	_____
14. _____	_____	_____	_____

III. TREND DATA

In order to find out what trends are common to many religious orders we need to have a clear picture of admissions and withdrawals during the years since Vatican II.

11. Please indicate whether the following information is for a province or a whole congregation. Check one:

    1. _____ province   2. _____ congregation

12. How many women entered religious life in your province (or congregation, if you are responding for an order with no provinces) in each of the following periods:*

	1966-1970	1971-1975	1976-1980
a. number entered	1. _____	2. _____	3. _____
b. number of these who made first commitment	1. _____	2. _____	3. _____
c. number of these who made perpetual commitment	1. _____	2. _____	3. _____
d. total in the congregation in initial commitment (in 1970, 1975, 1980)	1. _____	2. _____	3. _____
e. total in the congregation in perpetual commitment (in 1970, 1975, 1980)	1. _____	2. _____	3. _____

*Approximate numbers here are better than no numbers.

13. How many of the following kinds of buildings have come under the management of your province or congregation during the years:**

PART A:

	1965-1970	1971-1975	1976-1980
1. novitiate house	1. _____	1. _____	1. _____
2. house of study	2. _____	2. _____	2. _____
3. provincial house	3. _____	3. _____	3. _____
4. postulate	4. _____	4. _____	4. _____
5. infirmary	5. _____	5. _____	5. _____
6. vacation house	6. _____	6. _____	6. _____
7. house of formation	7. _____	7. _____	7. _____
8. prayer centers	8. _____	8. _____	8. _____

**If these buildings are shared across provinces simply indicate this in a note so we will not count them more than once.

Other (please specify):

10. _____	10. _____	10. _____	10. _____
11. _____	11. _____	11. _____	11. _____
12. _____	12. _____	12. _____	12. _____

13. **PART B:**

	Congregation-owned			Not Congregation-owned		
	1966 to 1970	1971 to 1975	1976 to 1980	1966 to 1970	1971 to 1975	1976 to 1980
1. elementary school	1. ___	1. ___	1. ___	1. ___	1. ___	1. ___
2. high school	2. ___	2. ___	2. ___	2. ___	2. ___	2. ___
3. junior college	3. ___	3. ___	3. ___	3. ___	3. ___	3. ___
4. college	4. ___	4. ___	4. ___	4. ___	4. ___	4. ___
5. hospital	5. ___	5. ___	5. ___	5. ___	5. ___	5. ___
6. orphanage	6. ___	6. ___	6. ___	6. ___	6. ___	6. ___
Other (specify):						
7. _____	7. ___	7. ___	7. ___	7. ___	7. ___	7. ___
8. _____	8. ___	8. ___	8. ___	8. ___	8. ___	8. ___

13. **PART C:** In the past 15 years congregations have transformed the functions of buildings. Have you done so with any of the following types:*

Transformed from:	No.	To:	No.
1. house of formation	_____	1a. retreat and/or con- ference centers	_____
		1b. other (specify):	
		_____	___
2. sister residence (convents)	_____	2. _____	___
		_____	___
3. school	_____	3. _____	___
_____	___	_____	___
_____	___	_____	___
4. mother house	_____	4. _____	___
_____	___	_____	___
_____	___	_____	___
5. Other _____	_____	5. _____	___

13. **PART D:** How many of the following kinds of buildings have left the management of your congregation (province) during the years:

	1966-1970	1971-1975	1976-1980
1. novitiate house	1. _____	1. _____	1. _____
2. house of study	2. _____	2. _____	2. _____

3. provincial house   3._____   3._____   3._____
4. postulate   4._____   4._____   4._____
5. infirmary   5._____   5._____   5._____
6. vacation house   6._____   6._____   6._____
7. house of formation   7._____   7._____   7._____
8. house of studies   8._____   8._____   8._____
9. prayer centers   9._____   9._____   9._____
Other (please specify):
10. _____   10._____   10._____   10._____
11. _____   11._____   11._____   11._____
12. _____   12._____   12._____   12._____

13. **PART E:**

	Congregation-owned			Not Congregation-owned		
	1966 to 1970	1971 to 1975	1976 to 1980	1966 to 1970	1971 to 1975	1976 to 1980
1. elementary school	1. __	1. __	1. __	1. __	1. __	1. __
2. high school	2. __	2. __	2. __	2. __	2. __	2. __
3. junior college	3. __	3. __	3. __	3. __	3. __	3. __
4. college	4. __	4. __	4. __	4. __	4. __	4. __
5. hospital	5. __	5. __	5. __	5. __	5. __	5. __
6. orphanage	6. __	6. __	6. __	6. __	6. __	6. __
Other (specify):						
7. _____	7. __	7. __	7. __	7. __	7. __	7. __
8. _____	8. __	8. __	8. __	8. __	8. __	8. __

*Include selling or renting.

14. Please indicate where changes in foundations took place in your province (or congregation, if no province) from:

	1966-1970			1971-1975		
	No. in central city	No. in suburbs	No. in rural areas	No. in central city	No. in suburbs	No. in rural areas
1. works or projects undertaken	1. __	1. __	1. __	1. __	1. __	1. __
2. works or projects discontinued	2. __	2. __	2. __	2. __	2. __	2. __

	1976-1980		
	No. in central city	No. in suburbs	No. in rural areas
1. works or projects undertaken	1. ___	1. ___	1. ___
2. works or projects discontinued	2. ___	2. ___	2. ___

IV. HEALTH

15. Do you have a specific retirement age?   1.___ yes   2.___ no

16. If yes, what is it now? _____
    What was it in 1966? _____

17. When did you introduce the current one? Year _____

18a. Are your eligible sisters registered for the Medicare program?
     1.___ yes   2.___ no

18b. Are your eligible sisters registered for the Medicaid program?
     1.___ yes   2.___ no

19a. Do you have a private health insurance program?
     1.___ yes   2.___ no

19b. Do you have a diocesan health insurance program?
     1.___ yes   2.___ no

19c. We have some other form of health insurance _____
     Please specify: _____

20. How many sisters do you have over 65 in your province (or congregation, if no provinces)?   _____ number over 65

21. How many sisters are inactive due to ill health or old age?

	ill health	old age
1. inactive	1._____	1._____

2. partially inactive, but still engaged in
   part-time work in the community
   (e.g. tutoring small groups, working
   in the house)   2._____ 2._____

V. SCREENING PROCEDURES

22. Because of the variety of results from experimentation with
    testing programs, we wish to gather the available information
    on what has been tried. Kindly check those spaces which apply
    in your case.

    1._____ We have never had a testing program prior to admis-
                    sions and are not planning to have one.
    2._____ We are planning such a program.
    3._____ We are just beginning our first program now.
    4._____ We had a program but have discontinued it.
    5._____ We have a program and expect to continue it.
    6._____ We have a program and are planning to discontinue it.
    7._____ We have a program and are reevaluating it.
    8._____ other (specify): _____

23. If you had a testing program but have discontinued it, how long
    did you have it and when did you discontinue it?
    a. _____ number of years   b. _____ date program terminated

24. Why did you discontinue it? _____
    _____

25. Which of the following types of tests are given to candidates
    applying to your congregation? Are they given to all candidates
    or just selected candidates? For how long have you used these
    tests? Please check as many categories as apply.

Type of Test	Candidates who are tested			No. of years used
	All	Most	Few	
1. IQ	1._____	2._____	3._____	1._____
2. Vocational Inventory	1._____	2._____	3._____	2._____
3. Standard Personality Test	1._____	2._____	3._____	3._____

4. Projective Test   1.____   2.____   3.____   4._____

5. College Entrance
   Examination   1.____   2.____   3.____   5._____

Other (specify):

6. _____   1.____   2.____   3.____   6._____

7. _____   1.____   2.____   3.____   7._____

8. _____   1.____   2.____   3.____   8._____

26. Please record here the code number (given in item 25) beside the tests listed above for those tests you have found most useful and those least useful. Include those you have added. (e.g. 1. IQ)

     Most Useful   **Least Useful**

     a. _____   a. _____

     b. _____   b. _____

     c. _____   c. _____

27. Which of the following types of interviews are given to candidates applying to your congregation? Please check as many categories as apply.

Interviews	Candidates who are interviewed			No. of Years used
	All	Most	Few	
1. Sister trained in psychology	1.____	2.____	3.____	1.____
2. Formation Director	1.____	2.____	3.____	2.____
3. Member of Governing Group	1.____	2.____	3.____	3.____
4. Vocation Director	1.____	2.____	3.____	4.____
5. Psychiatrist	1.____	2.____	3.____	5.____
6. Outside psychologist	1.____	2.____	3.____	6.____
Other (please specify):				
7. _____	1.____	2.____	3.____	7.____
8. _____	1.____	2.____	3.____	8.____

28. Please record here the code number (given in item 27) beside the interviews you have found most useful and those least useful. Include those you have added (e.g. 1. sister trained in psychology).

     Most Useful   **Least Useful**

     a. _____   a. _____

     b. _____   b. _____

     c. _____   c. _____

29. Which of the following types of credentials are requested from candidates applying to your congregation? Please check as many categories as apply.

Credentials	Candidates who are requested			No. of Years used
	All	Most	Few	
1. Recommendation from pastor	1.＿＿	2.＿＿	3.＿＿	1.＿＿＿
2. Recommendation from sister in community	1.＿＿	2.＿＿	3.＿＿	2.＿＿＿
3. Letter from someone who knows the family	1.＿＿	2.＿＿	3.＿＿	3.＿＿＿
4. Letter from business acquaintance of family	1.＿＿	2.＿＿	3.＿＿	4.＿＿＿
5. Letters from teachers	1.＿＿	2.＿＿	3.＿＿	5.＿＿＿
6. Visit to family	1.＿＿	2.＿＿	3.＿＿	6.＿＿＿
7. Letter from close friend	1.＿＿	2.＿＿	3.＿＿	7.＿＿＿
8. Letter from business acquaintance of candidate or professional associate	1.＿＿	2.＿＿	3.＿＿	8.＿＿＿
Other (specify):				
9. ＿＿＿＿＿＿	1.＿＿	2.＿＿	3.＿＿	9.＿＿＿
10. ＿＿＿＿＿＿	1.＿＿	2.＿＿	3.＿＿	10.＿＿＿

30. Please record here the code number (given in item 29) beside the types of credentials listed above for those types you have found most useful and those least useful. Include those you have added (e.g. 1. recommendation from pastor).

Most Useful   Least Useful
a. ＿＿＿＿＿＿   a. ＿＿＿＿＿＿
b. ＿＿＿＿＿＿   b. ＿＿＿＿＿＿
c. ＿＿＿＿＿＿   c. ＿＿＿＿＿＿

32. If you have a testing program please indicate who administers the test and who interprets the test. Put a (1) if the person always administers or always interprets the test. Put a (2) if the

person sometimes administers or sometimes interprets the test.
Mark as many categories as apply.

Administers	Interprets	
1._____	1._____	lay professional psychiatrist
2._____	2._____	lay professional psychologist
3._____	3._____	sister professional psychiatrist
4._____	4._____	sister professional psychologist
5._____	5._____	sister with some training in psychology
6._____	6._____	non-professional sister
7._____	7._____	vocation director
8._____	8._____	professional testing agency (e.g. CEEB service)
9._____	9._____	inter-community arrangements
10._____	10._____	other (specify): _____

33. Which of the following would usually be considered reasons for not accepting candidates? Check as many as apply.

	Always	Sometimes	Never
1. Illegitimacy	1._____	2._____	3._____
2. Marriage vows	1._____	2._____	3._____
3. Intellectual level	1._____	2._____	3._____
4. Disrupted family background	1._____	2._____	3._____
5. Age	1._____	2._____	3._____
6. Belonging to another rite	1._____	2._____	3._____
7. Divorce	1._____	2._____	3._____
8. Physical handicap	1._____	2._____	3._____

Other (specify):

	Always	Sometimes	Never
9. _____	1._____	2._____	3._____
10. _____	1._____	2._____	3._____

34. If there is a limitation in regard to intellectual level, what standards are required? _____

35. If there are restrictions in regard to age, what is the maximum age allowed? _____ Minimum? _____

36. What procedures do you follow for Sisters transferring from another congregation regarding interviews and tests?

_____ 1. the same as new candidates

_____ 2. other (please specify)

39. Who is consulted about all the candidates concerning their admission to the community? Please check as many as apply.

	Always	Sometimes	Never
1. Formation personnel	1. _____	2. _____	3. _____
2. Provincial council	1. _____	2. _____	3. _____
3. Professional psychiatrist	1. _____	2. _____	3. _____
4. Professional psychologist	1. _____	2. _____	3. _____
5. Medical doctor	1. _____	2. _____	3. _____
6. Spiritual director	1. _____	2. _____	3. _____
8. Vocation director	1. _____	2. _____	3. _____
9. Major superior (coordinator) (other than one accepting candidate)	1. _____	2. _____	3. _____

Other (specify):

	Always	Sometimes	Never
10. _____	1. _____	2. _____	3. _____
11. _____	1. _____	2. _____	3. _____
12. _____	1. _____	2. _____	3. _____

40. In the process of screening for the year 1981, how many candidates fall under the following categories?

1. _____ number of applicants
2. _____ number of acceptances
3. _____ number advised not to come
4. _____ number who actually came

41. Of those admitted in 1981, how many had the following backgrounds:

1. _____ No high school diploma
2. _____ High school diploma only
3. _____ Bachelor's degree
4. _____ Master's degree
5. _____ Doctoral degree
6. _____ Nursing degree
7. _____ Social work degree
8. _____ Professional degree other than nursing and social work (e.g. law). Please specify: _____
9. _____ Some college work
10. _____ Other special training of a post high school nature (but no degree)

42. Have you any special educational or experience requirement for entrance? Check as many as apply.

1. _____ high school diploma

2. _____ B.A. or equivalent
3. _____ other educational requirement
4. _____ some college work
5. _____ some employment experience
6. _____ other (specify): _____

43. If other educational requirement is checked (i.e. No. 3 above), please specify: _____

44. How long is your current formation program, 1980?

	Years	Months
1. aspirancy or candidacy	1._____	1._____
2. postulancy or affiliate period	2._____	2._____
3. novitiate	3._____	3._____
4. period of formal educational training prior to going out on assignment	4._____	4._____
5. time after promises or first vows to professional of perpetual vows	5._____	5._____

45. Have you made any substantial changes in the length of the training period in the past fifteen years? Please check below.

	Eliminated	Shortened	Extended	Revised	Initiated
1. aspirancy or candidacy	1. ___	1. ___	1. ___	1. ___	1. ___
2. pre-novitiate	2. ___	2. ___	2. ___	2. ___	2. ___
3. novitiate	3. ___	3. ___	3. ___	3. ___	3. ___
4. temporary commitment	4. ___	4. ___	4. ___	4. ___	4. ___
5. tertianship	5. ___	5. ___	5. ___	5. ___	5. ___

46. Please descibe briefly the changes made _____

47. Is there a special non-college program offered for those without college ability? 1._____ yes 2._____ no

48. If yes, please describe briefly: _____

49. In what fields of study do your sisters hold advanced degrees? Indicate the number of degrees completed and the number in process.

	Number of Masters		Number of Doctorates		Number of Bachelors	
	Comp	In Proc	Comp	In Proc	Comp	In Proc
1. Economics	1. _	1. _	1. _	1. _	1. _	1. _
2. Political Science	2. _	2. _	2. _	2. _	2. _	2. _
3. Psychology	3. _	3. _	3. _	3. _	3. _	3. _
4. Sociology	4. _	4. _	4. _	4. _	4. _	4. _
5. Anthropology	5. _	5. _	5. _	5. _	5. _	5. _
6. History	6. _	6. _	6. _	6. _	6. _	6. _
7. French	7. _	7. _	7. _	7. _	7. _	7. _
8. German	8. _	8. _	8. _	8. _	8. _	8. _
9. Italian	9. _	9. _	9. _	9. _	9. _	9. _
10. Latin	10. _	10. _	10. _	10. _	10. _	10. _
11. Spanish	11. _	11. _	11. _	11. _	11. _	11. _
12. Russian	12. _	12. _	12. _	12. _	12. _	12. _
13. Linguistics	13. _	13. _	13. _	13. _	13. _	13. _
14. Biology	14. _	14. _	14. _	14. _	14. _	14. _
15. Chemistry	15. _	15. _	15. _	15. _	15. _	15. _
16. Geography	16. _	16. _	16. _	16. _	16. _	16. _
17. Mathematics	17. _	17. _	17. _	17. _	17. _	17. _
18. Physics	18. _	18. _	18. _	18. _	18. _	18. _
19. Statistics	19. _	19. _	19. _	19. _	19. _	19. _
20. Art	20. _	20. _	20. _	20. _	20. _	20. _
21. Drama & Speech	21. _	21. _	21. _	21. _	21. _	21. _
22. Music	22. _	22. _	22. _	22. _	22. _	22. _
23. Literature	23. _	23. _	23. _	23. _	23. _	23. _
24. Philosophy	24. _	24. _	24. _	24. _	24. _	24. _
25. Law	25. _	25. _	25. _	25. _	25. _	25. _
26. Medical Technicians	26. _	26. _	26. _	26. _	26. _	26. _
27. Nursing & Nursing Ed	27. _	27. _	27. _	27. _	27. _	27. _
28. Doctor	28. _	28. _	28. _	28. _	28. _	28. _
29. Education	29. _	29. _	29. _	29. _	29. _	29. _
30. Social Work	30. _	30. _	30. _	30. _	30. _	30. _
31. Guidance and Counseling	31. _	31. _	31. _	31. _	31. _	31. _
32. Library Science	32. _	32. _	32. _	32. _	32. _	32. _
33. Administration	33. _	33. _	33. _	33. _	33. _	33. _
34. Theology/Religious Education	34. _	34. _	34. _	34. _	34. _	34. _

35. Business/Business
    Ed   35. _ 35. _   35. _ 35. _   35. _ 35. _
36. Fine Arts   36. _ 36. _   36. _ 36. _   36. _ 36. _
37. Science (General) 37. _ 37. _   37. _ 37. _   37. _ 37. _
38. Home Economics   38. _ 38. _   38. _ 38. _   38. _ 38. _
39. Special Education 39. _ 39. _   39. _ 39. _   39. _ 39. _
40. Journalism/
    Commercial Arts   40. _ 40. _   40. _ 40. _   40. _ 40. _

41. Afro-Amer.
    Studies   41. _ 41. _   41. _ 41. _   41. _ 41. _
42. Amer. Studies   42. _ 42. _   42. _ 42. _   42. _ 42. _
43. English   43. _ 43. _   43. _ 43. _   43. _ 43. _
44. Geography   44. _ 44. _   44. _ 44. _   44. _ 44. _
45. Greek   45. _ 45. _   45. _ 45. _   45. _ 45. _
46. Engineering   46. _ 46. _   46. _ 46. _   46. _ 46. _
47. Missiology   47. _ 47. _   47. _ 47. _   47. _ 47. _
48. Psychiatry   48. _ 48. _   48. _ 48. _   48. _ 48. _
49. Urban Studies   49. _ 49. _   49. _ 49. _   49. _ 49. _
50. Asian Studies   50. _ 50. _   50. _ 50. _   50. _ 50. _
51. Communication
    Arts   51. _ 51. _   51. _ 51. _   51. _ 51. _
52. New languages
    (e.g. Chinese)   52. _ 52. _   52. _ 52. _   52. _ 52. _
53. Advertising   53. _ 53. _   53. _ 53. _   53. _ 53. _
Other (specify):
54. _____   54. _ 54. _   54. _ 54. _   54. _ 54. _
55. _____   55. _ 55. _   55. _ 55. _   55. _ 55. _
56. _____   56. _ 56. _   56. _ 56. _   56. _ 56. _
57. _____   57. _ 57. _   57. _ 57. _   57. _ 57. _
58. _____   58. _ 58. _   58. _ 58. _   58. _ 58. _
59. _____   59. _ 59. _   59. _ 59. _   59. _ 59. _
60. _____   60. _ 60. _   60. _ 60. _   60. _ 60. _
61. _____   61. _ 61. _   61. _ 61. _   61. _ 61. _
62. _____   62. _ 62. _   62. _ 62. _   62. _ 62. _
63. _____   63. _ 63. _   63. _ 63. _   63. _ 63. _

50. From what universities or colleges have your sisters received
    degrees since 1965? Kindly name as many as you can recall.

No. of degrees   **Name of College/University**

1. _____   1. _____

2. _____   2. _____

3. _____   3. _____
4. _____   4. _____
5. _____   5. _____
6. _____   6. _____
7. _____   7. _____
8. _____   8. _____
9. _____   9. _____
10. _____   10. _____
11. _____   11. _____
12. _____   12. _____
13. _____   13. _____
14. _____   14. _____
15. _____   15. _____
16. _____   16. _____
17. _____   17. _____
18. _____   18. _____
19. _____   19. _____
20. _____   20. _____

51. How many sisters are currently released for full-time study on the graduate level?

_____ 1. studying but not for a degree
_____ 2. studying for a master's degree
_____ 3. studying for a doctor's degree
_____ 4. studying for other professional degree

52. How many sisters are currently doing part-time study on the graduate level?

_____ 1. studying but not for a degree
_____ 2. studying for a master's degree
_____ 3. studying for a doctor's degree
_____ 4. studying for other professional degree

53. How many sisters do you have trained or in training specifically for administrative work?

1. _____number already trained   2. _____number in training

53a. For what positions is this training?

1. Specific positions (please specify)

1. _____   4. _____
2. _____   5. _____
3. _____   6. _____

2. For no particular position _____ (check if applicable)

54. How many sisters do you have in training or already trained for specializations different from works you did prior to 1965?

Fields:	Number, if known
1. _____	_____
2. _____	_____
3. _____	_____
4. _____	_____
5. _____	_____
6. _____	_____
7. _____	_____
8. _____	_____
9. _____	_____
10. _____	_____

VI. SEPARATION

55a. How many sisters left your congregation in the years specified?

	Permanent Separation	
	Before Final Vows	After Final Vows
1. In 1966	1. _____	1. _____
2. In 1970	2. _____	2. _____
3. In 1976	3. _____	3. _____
4. In 1980	4. _____	4. _____

55b. Between 1966 and 1981, how many Sisters left your congregation? _____ No.

55c. How many sisters transferred into your congregation from another congregation between 1966 and 1981? _____

56. What do you consider the main reasons why sisters who have not yet made perpetual vows leave your congregation? Please check.

Reason for leaving	Very frequent	Frequent	Seldom	Never
1. No vocation	1. _____	2. _____	3. _____	4. _____
2. Weak formation	1. _____	2. _____	3. _____	4. _____
3. Preference for marriage	1. _____	2. _____	3. _____	4. _____
4. Dissatisfaction with community life	1. _____	2. _____	3. _____	4. _____

5. Interest in different
mode of apostolate   1. _____ 2. _____ 3. _____ 4. _____
6. Failure to achieve
personal fulfillment 1. _____ 2. _____ 3. _____ 4. _____
7. Psychological
disturbance   1. _____ 2. _____ 3. _____ 4. _____
8. Completion of pro-
fessional training   1. _____ 2. _____ 3. _____ 4. _____
9. No clear reasons   1. _____ 2. _____ 3. _____ 4. _____
10. New appreciation of
lay role   1. _____ 2. _____ 3. _____ 4. _____
11. Disenchantment with
direction of
community   1. _____ 2. _____ 3. _____ 4. _____
Other (specify):
12. _____ 1. _____ 2. _____ 3. _____ 4. _____
13. _____ 1. _____ 2. _____ 3. _____ 4. _____
14. _____ 1. _____ 2. _____ 3. _____ 4. _____

57. **What do you consider the main reasons why sisters who have
made perpetual vows leave your congregation? Please check.**

Reason for leaving	Very Frequent	Frequent	Seldom	Never
1. No vocation	1. _____	2. _____	3. _____	4. _____
2. Weak formation	1. _____	2. _____	3. _____	4. _____
3. Preference for marriage	1. _____	2. _____	3. _____	4. _____
4. Dissatisfaction with community life	1. _____	2. _____	3. _____	4. _____
5. Interest in different mode of apostolate	1. _____	2. _____	3. _____	4. _____
6. Failure to achieve personal fulfillment	1. _____	2. _____	3. _____	4. _____
7. Psychological disturbance	1. _____	2. _____	3. _____	4. _____
8. Completion of pro-fessional training	1. _____	2. _____	3. _____	4. _____
9. No clear reasons	1. _____	2. _____	3. _____	4. _____
10. New appreciation of lay role	1. _____	2. _____	3. _____	4. _____
11. Disenchantment with direction of community	1. _____	2. _____	3. _____	4. _____

Other (please specify):
12. _____ 1. _____ 2. _____ 3. _____ 4. _____
13. _____ 1. _____ 2. _____ 3. _____ 4. _____
14. _____ 1. _____ 2. _____ 3. _____ 4. _____

58. Of the sisters who have left your congregation in the past five years, how many were recommended by the congregation to leave? (Answer for your province or the entire congregation if there are no provinces.)
Number _____

VII. GOVERNMENT

63a. In which of the following ways are local superiors assigned to office? (If there are no local superiors, check here and proceed to the next question. No local superiors _____.) (If there are *some* local superiors, check here and respond to the question. Some local superiors _____.)

	Always	Sometimes	Never
1. chosen by local sisters	1. _____	2. _____	3. _____
2. chosen by Provincial officer(s) on the recommendations of local sisters	1. _____	2. _____	3. _____
3. chosen by Provincial officer(s) without recommendations	1. _____	2. _____	3. _____
4. appointed by the Congregational government officer(s) in consultation with Provincial officer(s)	1. _____	2. _____	3. _____
5. appointed by the Congregational government officer(s) without any specific consultation	1. _____	2. _____	3. _____

Other (please specify):

6. _____	1. _____	2. _____	3. _____
7. _____	1. _____	2. _____	3. _____
8. _____	1. _____	2. _____	3. _____

63b. If communities are collegial, how is local representation chosen?
_____ 1. elected locally
_____ 2. appointed
_____ 3. there is no set representation
_____ 4. Other (specify)

64. Have you any special training for newly appointed congregational administrators?

	In practice 15 years ago	In practice now
1. Always	1. _____	1. _____
2. Usually	2. _____	2. _____
3. Occasionally	3. _____	3. _____
4. Never	4. _____	4. _____

65. After the expiration of a given term of office does the administrator return to typical apostolic activities?

	In practice 15 years ago	In practice now
1. Always	1. _____	1. _____
2. Usually	2. _____	2. _____
3. Occasionally	3. _____	3. _____
4. Never	4. _____	4. _____

66. Are administrators of the congregation regarded de facto as principals of schools or administrators of hospitals or of other works related to the local place of appointment?

	In practice 15 years ago	In practice now
1. Always	1. _____	1. _____
2. Usually	2. _____	1. _____
3. Occasionally	3. _____	3. _____
4. Never	4. _____	4. _____

67. How are the local councillors selected for office? (We have no local councillors now _____.) (We have local councillors only in a few houses now _____.)

	Always	Sometimes	Never
1. chosen by local sisters	1. _____	2. _____	3. _____
2. chosen by Provincial officer(s) on the recommendations of local sisters	1. _____	2. _____	3. _____
3. chosen by Provincial officer(s) without recommendations	1. _____	2. _____	3. _____
4. appointed by the Congregational government officer(s) in consultation with Provincial officer(s)	1. _____	2. _____	3. _____
5. appointed by the Congregational goverment officer(s) without any specific consultation	1. _____	2. _____	3. _____

Other (specify):

6. _____ 1. _____ 2. _____ 3. _____
7. _____ 1. _____ 2. _____ 3. _____
8. _____ 1. _____ 2. _____ 3. _____

68. How do sisters represent their views in policy formation within the province (congregation) now? Please check.

	Most Usual	Accepted and quite usual	Accepted but unusual	Most Unusual	Never
1. by direct letter from sister to Administrator	1.___	2.___	3.___	4.___	5.___
2. by letter from several sisters to Provincial administrator	1.___	2.___	3.___	4.___	5.___
3. through a committee appointed just for this purpose	1.___	2.___	3.___	4.___	5.___
4. through a standing committee whose purpose it is to handle policy suggestions	1.___	2.___	3.___	4.___	5.___
5. no planned method	1.___	2.___	3.___	4.___	5.___
6. assemblies	1.___	2.___	3.___	4.___	5.___
7. forums	1.___	2.___	3.___	4.___	5.___

Other (specify):

	Most Usual	Accepted and quite usual	Accepted but unusual	Most Unusual	Never
8. _____	1.___	2.___	3.___	4.___	5.___
9. _____	1.___	2.___	3.___	4.___	5.___

69. How did sisters represent their views in policy formation within the province (congregation) 15 years ago? Please check.

	Most Usual	Accepted and quite usual	Accepted but unusual	Most Unusual	Never
1. by direct letter from sister to Administrator	1.___	2.___	3.___	4.___	5.___
2. by letter from several sisters to Provincial administrator	1.___	2.___	3.___	4.___	5.___

3. through a commit-
   tee appointed just
   for this purpose   1.____ 2.____ 3.____ 4.____ 5.____
4. through a standing
   committee whose
   purpose it is to
   handle policy
   suggestions   1.____ 2.____ 3.____ 4.____ 5.____
5. no planned method   1.____ 2.____ 3.____ 4.____ 5.____
6. assemblies   1.____ 2.____ 3.____ 4.____ 5.____
7. forums   1.____ 2.____ 3.____ 4.____ 5.____
Other (specify):
8. _____ 1.____ 2.____ 3.____ 4.____ 5.____
9. _____ 1.____ 2.____ 3.____ 4.____ 5.____

70. Does the province (or congregation if no provinces) have a Council or similar structure?

	Elected		Appointed	
	Yes	No	Yes	No
1. for local affairs (to address local houses)	1.____	2.____	1.____	2.____
2. for provincial affairs	1.____	2.____	1.____	2.____
3. for total congregational affairs	1.____	2.____	1.____	2.____

71. Which of the following procedures is used for chapter preparation in your congregation? (Skip if have no provinces.)

	15 years ago			Now		
	always	some times	never	always	some times	never
1. Provincial Chapter is preceded by local planning meetings that prepare proposals*	1.__	2.__	3.__	1.__	2.__	3.__
2. There is a Provincial Chapter for proposals and elections	1.__	2.__	3.__	1.__	2.__	3.__

3. There is no Pro-
vincial Chapter
for proposals, but
there is a Provin-
cial Chapter for
the election of del-
egates to the Gen-
eral Chapter   1. ___ 2. ___ 3. ___   1. ___ 2. ___ 3. ___
4. Other (specify):

_____ 1. ___ 2. ___ 3. ___   1. ___ 2. ___ 3. ___

*Please describe _____

72. In which of the following ways are Provincial Superiors assigned to office (if provinces)? (Omit if no provinces.)

	Always	Sometimes	Never
1. elected by all the members of the province	1. _____	2. _____	3. _____
2. elected by members of Provincial Chapter	1. _____	2. _____	3. _____
3. appointed by the major administrators from nominees submitted by all the members of the members of the province	1. _____	2. _____	3. _____
4. appointed by the major administrators in informed consultation with members of the province	1. _____	2. _____	3. _____
5. appointed by major adminstrator in consultation with her council	1. _____	2. _____	3. _____
6. appointed by major administrators without any specific consultation	1. _____	2. _____	3. _____
Other (specify):			
7. _____	1. _____	2. _____	3. _____
8. _____	1. _____	2. _____	3. _____

73. Which of the following kinds of information are solicited and considered by the Provincial Chapter (if there is one)?

	solicited			considered		
	always	some times	never	always	some times	never
1. suggestions from individual houses and from individual sisters	1. ___	2. ___	3. ___	1. ___	2. ___	3. ___
2. suggestions from individual sisters only	1. ___	2. ___	3. ___	1. ___	2. ___	3. ___
3. suggestions from individual houses only	1. ___	2. ___	3. ___	1. ___	2. ___	3. ___
4. suggestions from elected representatives only	1. ___	2. ___	3. ___	1. ___	2. ___	3. ___
5. suggestions from local planning groups	1. ___	2. ___	3. ___	1. ___	2. ___	3. ___
Other (specify):						
6. _____	1. ___	2. ___	3. ___	1. ___	2. ___	3. ___

74. Who constitutes the membership of the Provincial Chapter? (Omit if no provinces.)

	No. by election	No. by appointment	No. ex officio	No. by personal choice
1. Total number of sisters	1. _____	1. _____	1. _____	1. _____
2. Number of superiors only	2. _____	2. _____	2. _____	2. _____
3. Number of sisters with perpetual vows	3. _____	3. _____	3. _____	3. _____
4. Number of sisters with temporary vows	4. _____	4. _____	4. _____	4. _____
5. Outsiders	5. _____	5. _____	5. _____	5. _____
Other (specify):				
6. _____	6. _____	6. _____	6. _____	6. _____
7. _____	7. _____	7. _____	7. _____	7. _____

75. When was your last Provincial Chapter held? (Omit if no provinces.)

_____

76. When will your next Provincial Chapter be held? (Omit if no provinces.)

_____

77. Will this be a regular or a special Chapter? (Omit if no provinces.)

1._____ Regular   2._____ Special

78. How do local sisters participate in the election of the Superior General or president of the Congregation?

1. _____ indirectly through the election of representatives for the Provincial Chapter only

2. _____ indirectly through the election of representatives for the General Chapter

3. _____ direct vote but with no pre-discussion of candidates

4. _____ planned consideration of candidates prior to direct vote

5. _____ other (specify): _____

_____

79. At present, how do the local sisters present their ideas for a General Chapter? (Check as many as apply.)

1. _____ A formal structure exists for communitcation between sisters and representatives

2. _____ No formal structure but communication among sisters and representatives is encouraged

3. _____ Sisters are asked to submit proposals to the chapter committees

4. _____ Sisters are asked to fill out questionnaires which survey their views

5. _____ Other (specify): _____

81. Which of the following kinds of information were considered at your last General Chapter?

	Major issue	Minor issue	No issue at all
1. Membership trends	1. _____	2. _____	3. _____
2. Choice of ministry	1. _____	2. _____	3. _____
3. Corporate mission	1. _____	2. _____	3. _____
4. Ownership of property	1. _____	2. _____	3. _____
5. Quality of community life	1. _____	2. _____	3. _____

6. Spiritual direction   1. _____ 2. _____ 3. _____
7. New direction of ministry   1. _____ 2. _____ 3. _____
8. Divestment   1. _____ 2. _____ 3. _____
9. Racism in places where you
   work   1. _____ 2. _____ 3. _____
10. Pastoral ministry for women   1. _____ 2. _____ 3. _____
11. Taking a congregational stand
    on disarmament   1. _____ 2. _____ 3. _____
12. Chemical dependency services   1. _____ 2. _____ 3. _____
13. Uses of testing services   1. _____ 2. _____ 3. _____
14. Retreat programs   1. _____ 2. _____ 3. _____
15. Declining finances   1. _____ 2. _____ 3. _____
16. Cost of housing   1. _____ 2. _____ 3. _____
17. Simple life styles   1. _____ 2. _____ 3. _____
18. Justice agenda of Church   1. _____ 2. _____ 3. _____
19. Health programs   1. _____ 2. _____ 3. _____
Other (specify):
20. _____   1. _____ 2. _____ 3. _____
21. _____   1. _____ 2. _____ 3. _____

82. Did your last General Chapter receive any pressing requests for changes or programs from groups of members?

    1. _____ yes   2. _____ no

83. If yes, on what issues? _____
    _____
    _____

84. In what form was the chapter reported to the members?

	Complete Report	Selected Report
1. a report to each sister	1. _____	2. _____
2. a report to each house	1. _____	2. _____
3. a report to each province, and then to the houses at the will of the provincial	1. _____	2. _____
Other (specify):		
4. _____	1. _____	2. _____
5. _____	1. _____	2. _____

85. When was your last General Chapter held? _____

86. When will your next General Chapter be held? _____

87. Will this be a regular or special chapter?

    1. _____ Regular   2. _____ Special

88. Looking back over the years since 1965 at the forms the special General Chapter(s) has (have) taken, what do you think will characterize your next General Chapter? In this response *compare the next one with those prior to 1966.* Please check the columns that are relevant and add what is not provided.

	Plan to do this	Plan not to do this	No Plans
1. More members will be present as delegates.	1. _____	2. _____	3. _____
2. The sessions will be open to non-delegates as observers.	1. _____	2. _____	3. _____
3. Representatives of the people we serve and work with will attend.	1. _____	2. _____	3. _____
4. It will be no longer than one week.	1. _____	2. _____	3. _____
5. It will be preceded by retreat days.	1. _____	2. _____	3. _____
6. It will focus more on issues of social justice.	1. _____	2. _____	3. _____
7. There will be orientation sessions, study days, consultants.	1. _____	2. _____	3. _____
Other (specify):			
8. _____	1. _____	2. _____	3. _____
9. _____	1. _____	2. _____	3. _____
10. _____	1. _____	2. _____	3. _____

89. How does your current General Chapter preparation differ from the preparation of earlier chapters?

    1. _____ a great deal   2. _____ somewhat   3. _____ not at all

90. How is representation distributed by region?

    _____

    _____

    _____

91. Of the total membership of the General Chapter, what is the percent of ex officio members and elected delegates?

    1. _____ total members   2. _____% ex officio   3. _____% elected

92. Will the representation at the next General Chapter be similar to Chapters prior to Vatican II?

   1._____ yes   2._____ no

93. If no, please check the ways in which the representation at your next General Chapter will be different:
   1. _____ general membership will be enlarged
   2. _____ number of elected delegates will be increased
   3. _____ method for electing delegates will be changed
   Other (specify):
   4. _____
   5. _____

   (Please respond to both item #94 and item #95)

94. How many professed sisters are there in your entire congregation? (Include all sisters who have made vows, even those who have only made their first vows, or promises.) Number: ___
   We have no provinces _____

95. If provinces, what is the total number of sisters in your province? (Include all sisters who have made vows, even those who have only made their first vows, or promises.) Number: ___ We have no provinces _____

VIII. CHANGE

96.

	All houses			Some houses			No houses
	always	some-times	never	always	some-times	never	
1. as much as possible, traditional style is retained.	1. __	2. __	3. __	1. __	2. __	3. __	4. __
2. In general, church renewals are carried out	1. __	2. __	3. __	1. __	2. __	3. __	4. __
3. There is daily liturgy.	1. __	2. __	3. __	1. __	2. __	3. __	4. __
Other (specify):							
4. _____	1. __	2. __	3. __	1. __	2. __	3. __	4. __
5. _____	1. __	2. __	3. __	1. __	2. __	3. __	4. __
6. _____	1. __	2. __	3. __	1. __	2. __	3. __	4. __

97. What kinds of retreat are available for sisters annually?

	15 years ago			Now		
	always	some times	never	always	some times	never
1. directed retreats planned for groups of sisters	1. ___	2. ___	3. ___	1. ___	2. ___	3. ___
2. local community sponsored	1. ___	2. ___	3. ___	1. ___	2. ___	3. ___
3. private directed retreats	1. ___	2. ___	3. ___	1. ___	2. ___	3. ___
4. private non-directed retreats	1. ___	2. ___	3. ___	1. ___	2. ___	3. ___
Other (specify):						
5. _____	1. ___	2. ___	3. ___	1. ___	2. ___	3. ___
6. _____	1. ___	2. ___	3. ___	1. ___	2. ___	3. ___

98. What qualities do you look for in persons you choose to direct your formation program? Select your first five preferences.

Qualities:

1. knowledge of theology
2. understanding of human psychology
3. deeply rooted in the tradition of the congregation
4. orientated toward innovation in the liturgy
5. orientated toward innovation in styles of community
6. concerned with the preservation of the congregation's customs and ideas
7. regularity of life
8. orderliness of personal effects
9. a splendid generosity
10. a justice orientation and experience
11. the mission of the church
12. sense of humor

Other (please specify):

13. _____
14. _____

Preferences:

1. _____
2. _____
3. _____
4. _____
5. _____

99. Do you seek the same qualities in your formation personnel now that were looked for 15 years ago in your congregation's formation program?

1. _____ yes   2. _____ no

100. If no, what is the difference? _____
_____

101. How are your formation personnel selected?

	Always	Sometimes	Never
1. appointed by the General Government with recommendation of Provincial Administrator	1. _____	2. _____	3. _____
2. appointed by the General Government with recommendation by Provincial council or province	1. _____	2. _____	3. _____
3. appointed by the General Government after informal discussions with persons of their own selection	1. _____	2. _____	3. _____
4. appointed by provincial government	1. _____	2. _____	3. _____
Other (specify):			
5. _____	1. _____	2. _____	3. _____
6. _____	1. _____	2. _____	3. _____

IX. MISCELLANEOUS

102. Do your sisters keep their own names as their religious names? (baptismal and surname)
1. _____ have always used their own names
2. _____ plan to change to use of own names
3. _____ most have changed to use of own names
4. _____ new sisters use their own names
5. _____ have not considered the use of own name
6. _____ individuals make the choice of use of names

103. What is the year for the revision of your constitutions that will be submitted to Rome for approval?
1. _____ Already done. Year _____.
2. _____ Coming.   Expected year _____.

104. Has there been a major revision (revisions) of your Rule or Constitutions in the last 15 years?   1. _____ yes 2. _____ no

105. If yes, what year (years)?   1. _____ 2. _____ 3. _____

106. Are you planning another revision of your Rule or Constitution?
   1. _____ yes   2. _____ no

107. If yes, approximately when? _____ .

108. If yes, what major changes do you have in mind? Proposed constitutional changes: _____

_____

_____

110. Are you reassessing your methods of missioning sisters in new works?   1. _____ yes   2. _____ no

111. If yes, will you describe the direction in which you plan to move or have already moved. Plans for new methods of placement:

_____

112a. Have there been changes in your religious habit in the past 15 years?
   1. _____ none
   2. _____ minor changes
   3. _____ major changes
   4. _____ we no longer have a religious habit

112b. Do you have a religious symbol?
   1. _____ yes
   2. _____ we have one and do not require it
   3. _____ we have a habit but no symbol
   4. _____ we have neither habit nor symbol

113. Are you planning changes in your religious habit in the next five years?
   1. _____ none
   2. _____ minor changes
   3. _____ major changes
   4. _____ we no longer have a religious habit

114. If there have been changes in your religious habit in the last five years, by whom were the decisions made to effect the change?

	decision to change	choice of style
1. by the major superior alone	1._____	2._____
2. by the major superior in consultation with her council	1._____	2._____

3. at a chapter but with no previous
    consultation with the sisters   1. _____   2. _____
4. at a chapter with a previous polling
    of all the sisters   1. _____   2. _____
5. by the direct vote of the entire
    congregation   5. _____   5. _____
    Other (specify):
6. _____ 6. _____   6. _____

115. What changes have been undertaken within the last 15 years
     regarding lifestyle in local communities? Check relevant
     columns.

	major changes	minor changes	no changes
1. horarium	1. _____	2. _____	3. _____
2. silence	1. _____	2. _____	3. _____
3. recreation	1. _____	2. _____	3. _____
4. chapter of faults	1. _____	2. _____	3. _____
5. participation in extra-community activities	1. _____	2. _____	3. _____
7. joining local neighborhood groups	1. _____	2. _____	3. _____
8. opening house to others	1. _____	2. _____	3. _____
9. encouraging friendships	1. _____	2. _____	3. _____
10. using personal budgets, community budgets, etc.	1. _____	2. _____	3. _____
11. having community decision making	1. _____	2. _____	3. _____
Other (specify):			
12. _____	1. _____	2. _____	3. _____
13. _____	1. _____	2. _____	3. _____

116. Looking forward to the next ten years, which of the following
     developments do you expect to see?

	No	Yes	Uncertain
1. an increase in the number of vocations	1. _____	2. _____	3. _____
2. continued expansion of foundations	1. _____	2. _____	3. _____
3. continuation of essentially the same works	1. _____	2. _____	3. _____
4. more involvement in civic and national programs	1. _____	2. _____	3. _____

5. more involvement in public
   protests   1. _____ 2. _____ 3. _____
6. greater voice for sisters in
   planning   1. _____ 2. _____ 3. _____
7. basic changes in types of work
   in education   1. _____ 2. _____ 3. _____
8. basic changes in types of work
   in health   1. _____ 2. _____ 3. _____
9. basic changes in types of work
   in welfare   1. _____ 2. _____ 3. _____
10. basic changes in style of reli-
    gious life   1. _____ 2. _____ 3. _____
11. none of these   1. _____ 2. _____ 3. _____
Other (specify):
12. _____ 1. _____ 2. _____ 3. _____
13. _____ 1. _____ 2. _____ 3. _____
14. _____ 1. _____ 2. _____ 3. _____

117. Which of the following kinds of reading is customarily encouraged for members?

1. _____ Bible reading   6. _____ diocesan paper
2. _____ news magazines   7. _____ spiritual readers
3. _____ news commentaries   8. _____ professional journals
4. _____ religious journals   Other (specify):
5. _____ daily newspaper   9. _____
                                10. _____

118. Which of the following news media would you recommend or encourage your sisters to read?

	Very Highly	highly	Moderately	Not at all
1. Sunday New York Times Magazine	1. _____	2. _____	3. _____	4. _____
2. Time	1. _____	2. _____	3. _____	4. _____
3. Newsweek	1. _____	2. _____	3. _____	4. _____
4. U.S. News and World Report	1. _____	2. _____	3. _____	4. _____
5. New Republic	1. _____	2. _____	3. _____	4. _____
6. National Review	1. _____	2. _____	3. _____	4. _____
7. National Catholic Reporter	1. _____	2. _____	3. _____	4. _____
8. Commonweal	1. _____	2. _____	3. _____	4. _____
9. America	1. _____	2. _____	3. _____	4. _____
10. Origins	1. _____	2. _____	3. _____	4. _____

11. Justice issue journals   1. _____ 2. _____ 3. _____ 4. _____
12. Sojourners   1. _____ 2. _____ 3. _____ 4. _____
13. Diocesan paper   1. _____ 2. _____ 3. _____ 4. _____
14. Literary journals   1. _____ 2. _____ 3. _____ 4. _____
Other (specify):
15. _____ 1. _____ 2. _____ 3. _____ 4. _____
16. _____ 1. _____ 2. _____ 3. _____ 4. _____
17. _____ 1. _____ 2. _____ 3. _____ 4. _____
18. _____ 1. _____ 2. _____ 3. _____ 4. _____
19. _____ 1. _____ 2. _____ 3. _____ 4. _____

119. What new works have you added to your apostolic activities in the past 5 years which you consider oriented to the expectations expressed in the Pastoral Constitution on the Church in the Modern World (1966) and Justice in the World (1971)?

New Works:

1. _____
2. _____
3. _____
4. _____
5. _____

120. Check the following conditions which you regard as barriers to the effective development of new roles for your sisters.
   1. _____ lack of preparation   5. _____ age
   2. _____ pressure of time due to   6. _____ lack of receptivity
        current works   7. _____ Church regulations
   3. _____ community customs   Other (specify):
   4. _____ lack of awareness of   8. _____
        contemporary situation

121. Check the following conditions which you regard as barriers to the effective development of the present roles filled by your sisters.
   1. _____ lack of preparation   5. _____ age
   2. _____ pressure of time due to   6. _____ lack of receptivity
        current works   7. _____ Church regulations
   3. _____ community customs   Other (specify):
   4. _____ lack of awareness of   8. _____
        contemporary situation

122. Which of the following sources do you perceive will be the major determinants of changes you will make in the next 5 years? Put a (4) beside that which you consider very influential in regard to change; put a (3) beside that which is less influential; put a (2) beside that which is somewhat influential; put a (1) beside that which is of minor influence.

   1. _____ the ideas of the sisters
   2. _____ the directives of the Sacred Congregation of Religious
   3. _____ the original intentions of the founder of the congregation
   4. _____ the decrees of Vatican II
   5. _____ the needs of the human community
   6. _____ human rights issues
   7. _____ women's issues
   8. _____ global perspective
   Other (specify):
   9. _____

123. Which of the following do you perceive as the most pressing needs of this moment? Put (4) (3) (2) (1) as in directions in item 122 above.

   1. _____ cooperation with the directives from the Sacred Congregation
   2. _____ circumspection in administrators and patience in subjects
   3. _____ intensification of efforts to achieve personal sanctity
   4. _____ careful study of society
   5. _____ careful study of theological developments
   6. _____ constant effort to open channels of communication
   7. _____ greater appreciation on the part of young religious for the achievements of the past
   8. _____ intense examination of the relevancy of the gospel to the current conditions of the world
   9. _____ deeper knowledge of the spirit of the founder
   10. _____ development of a basically new liturgical life
   11. _____ experiments with new kinds of community life
   12. _____ social justice
   13. _____ critical social analysis
   14. _____ action on behalf of oppressed and marginalized people

124. Are you trying any new ways of living community life?
     1. _____ yes   2. _____ no

125. If yes, please describe: _____
     _____
     _____

126. Have you introduced any new works?   1._____yes 2._____no

127. If yes, please describe and indicate how many of your sisters the change will effect. Changes: _____
     _____
     _____

128a. If your congregation has divided into provinces or regions or areas within the last 15 years, please indicate the year in which this occurred. Year: _____. What led to this decision?
      _____
      _____

128b. If your congregation has eliminated or reduced its provinces, regions or areas, please indicate how.
      1. _____ reduced.   Year: _____
      2. _____ eliminated.   Year: _____
      What led to this decision? _____
      _____

132. Where and when was your religious order founded?
     1. Country: _____
     2. Year: _____

133. Where is your motherhouse presently located? _____

134. Whom do you consider to be your founder(s)?
     1. _____
     2. _____

135. What do you consider to be the main problems facing religious congregations today? _____
     _____
     _____
     _____
     _____

THANK YOU FOR COMPLETING THIS DOCUMENT

Please use back page for any explanations you feel are necessary. Indicate the item to which you are referring.

Should you need further explanation, write or call:

LCWR RESEARCH	(617) 277-9340, Ext. 187
Sociology Dept.	Monday, 9:00-12:00
Emmanuel College	Wednesday, 9:00-4:30
Boston, Mass. 02115	Friday, 9:00-4:30

Patricia O'Brien, SND de Namur
Marie Augusta Neal, SND de Namur

KINDLY RETURN THIS COMPLETED DOCUMENT
TO THE ADDRESS INDICATED ABOVE